INTUITIVELY
YOU

EVOLVE YOUR LIFE AND
MEND THE WORLD

About the Author

Michelle's mission is to educate the world about the power of intuition to solve our personal, social, economical and philosophical life issues.

Michelle believes Americans specifically have a unique opportunity to change the global status quo by learning the science of inner wisdom to achieve not only personal balance but collective harmony.

"With intuition's ability to heighten our perceptions beyond our ego-driven needs for validation, we become more understanding, accepting and peaceful, wanting for the greater good as much as we want for ourselves."

- Michelle DesPres

Help Michelle change the world . . . learn to be intuitive!

Credentials

Michelle is a certified clairvoyant medium trained under the Berkeley Psychic Institute program for inner development. She is also the author of the books, *The Clairvoyant Path*, and *INTUITIVELY YOU*, helping others discover personal and collective fulfillment. Michelle also drafted the *Intuitive Ethical Standards*, establishing industry guidelines for alternative therapists.

Michelle is a frequent speaker and motivational leader. She has been providing individual services and readings to a diversity of clients for 15 years, who treasure her insight, perspective and deeply nurturing guidance. She is the founder of the Intuitive Practitioner Program, teaching students about mind, body and soul integration – and how to hone these skills to build thriving businesses.

Learn More and Contact Michelle

www.MichelleDesPres.com

INTUITIVELY
YOU

EVOLVE YOUR LIFE AND
MEND THE WORLD

MICHELLE DESPRES
THE ETHICAL INTUITIVE™

Triple Three Press, Denver, Colorado www.triplethreepress.com

While these are the stories of Michelle's clients and personal experiences, all names and some details have been changed to maintain privacy.

Publisher's Cataloging-in-Publication Data

Names: DesPres, Michelle, 1968- author.
Title: Intuitively you : evolve your life and mend the world / Michelle DesPres.
Description: Lakewood, CO : Triple Three Press, 2019. |
    Summary: Presents a step-by-step pathway to the intuitive
    lifestyle, meant to capture fundamental intuitive powers and
    enhance the reader's life journey.
Identifiers: LCCN 2018914272 | ISBN 9781732903906 (pbk.) |
    ISBN 9781732903913 (ebook) | ISBN 9781732903920
    (audible)
Subjects: LCSH: Intuition. | Mind and body. | Self-actualization
(Psychology). | BISAC: SELF-HELP /   Personal Growth /
General.
Classification: LCC BF315.5.D47 2019 (print) | LCC BF315.5 (ebook) | DDC
153.44--dc23
LC record available at https://lccn.loc.gov/2018914272

Ordering Information:

Quantity sales. Special discounts are available on quantity purchases by corporations, associations, and others. For details, contact the Special Sales Department at the web address above.

Intuitively You / Michelle E. DesPres.1st ed.

Print: 978-1-7329039-0-6
eBook: 978-1-7329039-1-3
Mobi: 978-1-7329039-3-7
Audible Book 978-1-7329039-2-0

CONTENTS

ACKNOWLEDGEMENTS

Roger Lee Freeman

Your unwavering empathy, patience, deep wisdom, and immense help in conceptualizing this project are the only reasons this book exists. I am so lucky to have you on my side. The world has never been brighter than with you in my heart.

Gaye Lundgren

Unconditional love is a gift few can give yet you somehow offer it with joy and abundance. Your friendship and generosity has forever changed my ability to create higher circumstances for myself. Thank you for always believing in me.

CONTRIBUTING EDITORS

Ralph Henley
Jane Nicolet
Myrna James Yoo

DEDICATED TO

Rena Lynn

INTRODUCTION

Intuition Leads Humanity to Higher Purpose

"You cannot fix the problem with the same thinking that created the problem."

— Albert Einstein, Theoretical Physicist

I WAS VISITING my daughter-in-law recently, when she gave me a gift that confirmed my greatest wishes. She had been shopping in a prominent department store and saw a black sleeveless t-shirt that reminded her of me. As I unfolded the garment, I was shocked at what I read. Imprinted on the front in large gold and white letters was the phrase, "FOLLOW YOUR INTUITION." Retailers are notorious for hopping on bandwagons and following trends. If they believed the higher senses were an ideal worth promoting, it must be on everyone's mind. That's when I knew life wouldn't be the same again . . . it would be better!

Did you know that in February 2017, *Forbes* magazine reported that intuition is the highest form of intelligence and listed it as one of the top ten qualities of all great leaders? With companies like Apple, Inc., which often refers to their products as being intuitive, and the American Express Company, which is writing articles on how intuition can take your business to the next level, it's clear that what was once a fringe notion has finally cycled into mainstream thinking! More importantly, our perceptual shift in thinking signals that we have entered a period of great change with the power to transform our personal lives and the world into higher, more purposeful expressions.

- What if you could use your higher perspective to heal yourself, all your relationships, and even your sense of purpose?

- What if you could use your inner senses to bring balance and peace to the world?

You may not be aware of it, but the greatest opportunity of your life and the future of humanity are in your hands, or rather in your ability to see from an expanded point of view.

There is little debate that as a species we are at a crossroads. Humanity can destroy itself through war and its environment through ignorance, or it can choose to evolve its thinking and find higher solutions to the world's most dire issues. My bet is on evolution. In fact, I've been seeing advancement for years.

Alternative concepts such as herbal medicine, past-life regression, reiki and even psychic-mediumship are no longer considered outlandish practices. Rather, these healing alternatives have intuitively cycled into the conventional mindset, leading many people to increased healing, empowerment and ability to affect positive change in the world.

Albert Einstein was correct in saying that you cannot solve a problem with the same thinking that created it. If you use the lower mind to resolve an issue, you will experience lesser results. However, when you approach your life's challenges with a higher perspective, you generate greater personal and collective outcomes. Intuition is our evolved thinking. Better yet, it's no longer reserved for only a "gifted" few… everyone is intuitive!

Intuition isn't a new concept – it simply hasn't received its proper credit. I know many people who have invested in counseling and coaching programs, hoping to receive life guidance, only to inevitably be told to trust their gut or to follow their heart – which really means be intuitive with yourself. We simply don't call gut feelings intuition. More importantly, we don't teach individuals how to use their core instincts as a way of finding higher solutions to their life issues. As a result, most people have no idea that they are intuitive, let alone know how to trust their inner promptings to better themselves and the world. Thankfully, learning to use your higher senses is fun and easy. You just have to ask yourself:

- Am I willing to use what is already inside me to grow beyond my anxieties, addictions and limitations?

- Am I ready to discover my inner senses and live a sustainable life of improved health, transparent relationships, and meaningful purpose?

- Can I be open to innovative perspectives that have the power to shift the cultural ideals away from fear, greed, and war toward love, cooperation, innovation, and working in harmony with one another and our environment?

If you answered yes to any of these questions, this book will provide you with the tools you need to be INTUITIVELY YOU so you can evolve your life and mend the world.

It's a pleasure to be with you on your journey,

Michelle

WHY I WROTE THIS BOOK

A Departure from Higher Knowing

BEFORE DIVING INTO the wealth of information contained in this book, I would like to share with you my personal intuitive story. I shudder to think what my life might look like had I never embarked on such a transformative journey and feel certain you will relate to my plight as it likely mirrors your own.

As a young girl, I did not have a positive self-image. Most of the time, I felt unwanted and unloved. My mother was in the habit of using inappropriate, hateful words as a means of parenting my older sister and me. Consequently, I was an exceptionally introverted child who spent her time outdoors speaking to mountains, clouds, trees and imaginary friends more than real people. The messages I received from nature's spirit brought me peace and comfort unlike anything else in my life. I recall once when I was five years old going to the park by myself. That day I would have a profoundly psychic experience that I wouldn't realize was such for nearly three decades.

I was a year younger than most of the kids in my neighborhood and hadn't started school yet. So when everyone got onto the big yellow bus, I informed my mother that I would be at the park and started out on my solo journey. Of course, in the 70s, no one thought twice about letting small children roam unaccompanied. Except … I wasn't actually alone.

Above me, formed by clouds, was an Indian Squaw who watched over me the entire day. I can still remember her features with great detail, as if it were yesterday. She wore a straight leather dress with fringe at the bottom and moccasins on her feet. Her hair was long, braided and hanging over both shoulders. She even had a papoose on her back with a baby in it who was sleeping. For hours, the Native American mother hovered about, talking lovingly to me and keeping an eye on me as I played on the swings, singing songs to her and her infant.

That day was one of the best I can remember. It has only been as an adult that I've come to think of this experience as odd. To me as a child, it seemed natural, and I assumed this was how everyone communicated. Unfortunately, when I was old enough to share my etheric interactions with my friends, I realized that something about my perceptions was different.

One day while walking to school with a group of friends, I shared a strange dream I'd had about spirits and otherworldly things. After confiding what I thought was something ordinary, one of the girls stopped dead in her tracks, looked at me and said, "you're weird." In that moment of feeling awkward and dejected, I realized no one else communicated with the energetic world like me. It was then at age eight, that I learned to disassociate from my intuitive abilities in an effort to be like my peers. Unfortunately, discarding my ability to commune with the energetic world inadvertently worsened my already weakened sense of self.

The results of growing up were not pretty. My sister left home at seventeen, following a path of alcoholism, addiction and mental illness. I left home at fifteen, following the path of teen motherhood, which, honestly, made me the lucky one.

Motherhood momentarily saved me. Although it was a difficult path, being a mother centered me and gave me purpose. I had the love of my child, and with that bond, I managed to eke out a successful life. I finished my education, got a good-paying corporate job, and established a committed relationship just as society expected of me. By all standards, I had overcome my lesser circumstances and was living the American Dream. Except twenty years down that road, I found myself in severe distress.

I loathed my oil and gas corporate career. Not only did I feel I was contributing to the demise of people and planet, but the "good old boy" nepotism within the industry was proving to be a treacherous place for a woman. Then there was the issue of my marriage and how my value as a partner was directly related to the amount of income I did or didn't earn each month. The only thing I enjoyed was being a mother, although I never felt I had enough time with my children and was allowing money and status to take precedence over their better interests. It didn't make sense to me how living to the expectations of a lifestyle that seemed unrealistic, superficial and oppressive could be considered a dream. Surely, there was more to life than acquiring things? Or was my mother correct in saying happiness didn't exist – a notion I had always rejected and vowed to prove wrong?

I'm a minimalist by nature. In many ways, a roof over my head is all I need. Unfortunately, no one in my life or within our cultural messaging shared my beliefs. Fulfillment to me meant fostering love, connection, nurturing and healing. Yet, a well-lived life to those around me, and on every commercial on television, suggested that living in a palatial home, driving the most luxurious car, owning sixty pairs of shoes, and escaping to exotic lands and trampling the landscape was the life one should aspire to live.

Unfortunately, try as I might to assert my way of being, I hadn't been able to break society's programming and create a lifestyle that reflected my ideals. I was depressed. It seemed that my only hopes for happiness were to live a Prozac-induced life or learn to meditate. While meditation was great for releasing pent-up frustrations, it did little to change my outward circumstances, leaving pharmaceuticals as my only option. Except medicating myself was never really something I could do. I wasn't willing to mask my unhappiness just for the sake of living to mediocrity. It seemed that I had no good alternatives.

My Intuitive Solution

My life was falling apart. Something needed to change. I had decided that change would be my marriage, although I knew the problem was bigger than our relationship. In many ways, I was the issue. Yes, my worth as a partner seemed marginalized, but that was only because I was lost. As an individual, I had forgotten who I was. I was good at pretending to be what I was instructed to be, but had no idea how to be myself. The consequences of living a make-believe life created a sense of depression and anger within me.

Thankfully, the unseen world would once again befriend me despite having put them on a shelf, giving me the hope I desperately needed.

One day while sad, in tears and contemplating the end of what I had dreamed would be a love forever, I heard a woman say to me, "Fret not, everything will be fine." I spun around expecting to see someone standing in my home, but much to my surprise, I was alone. I realized that the voice was coming to me like telepathy – a thought projected to me by another person – but who and why?

I laughed at myself, thinking I was going crazy and hearing voices. Except her words were not just comforting, they were familiar. Her voice was the same as the Indian in the clouds who had watched over me as a child. She had come to remind me that I had lost touch with my inner guidance, and because of that, my life was in disarray. Although it was too late to save my marriage, it wasn't too late to save myself.

After hearing the woman speak to me, I again began having conversations with the etheric world in an attempt to glean their wisdom and discover my happiness. I also began reading everything I could about the subjects of energy and spirit, as I found comfort in knowing I was not the only person experiencing a different perceptual reality. Psychic medium John Edwards was one of my early influences, followed by Rosemary Altea, Sonia Choquette, Edgar Cayce, and Shakti Gawain. I also read Wayne Dyer, Deepak Chopra and quantum scientists such as Lynne McTaggart, Gregg Braden, and Masaru Emoto. However, it wasn't until I found a program teaching clairvoyant development that I was able to put all the esoteric theories I was learning into tangible, everyday practice.

I discovered a school in Denver that taught Lewis Bostwick's Berkeley Psychic Institute's Clairvoyant Program.[i] The course had been in existence for thirty years but was new to me. I quickly enrolled and began my formal intuitive education, reconnecting to my inner wisdom. Consequently, empowerment and the ability to find innovative solutions to my everyday issues with family, career, parenting, etc. suddenly become a reality, and my life finally began to make sense and feel worthwhile.

Living intuitively taught me who I was, why I was, and what my life's purpose could be. It not only allowed me to transcend my limited upbringing, toxic relationships, and destructive patterns, but helped me find purpose and a sense of belonging. Today I have a thriving family, a meaningful career, a deeply connected partnership and an unwavering knowing that intuition is the key to saving humanity.

An Intuitive World

"Intuition is less about suddenly 'knowing' the right answer and more about instinctively understanding information."

— *Forbes*, February 2017 [ii]

Notable scientists around the world are discovering what mystics and metaphysicians have said for eons. For instance, Dr. Michio Kaku, co-founder of the String Field Theory,[iii] supports the idea that all things are interconnected. Dr. Lynne McTaggart and her intention experiments demonstrate that thoughts create reality, and Dr. Masaru Emoto's water intention experiments show the power of intention to change the physical world. Thanks to these cutting-edge scientists, what used to be fringe thinking is now at the center of certain scientific research and is now referred to in conference rooms around the world. As a result, these revolutionary develop-ments are rapidly changing how we view and live our lives. There is no doubt about it. You are intuitive, and as such, you are a commodity in high demand with the power to forge a healthy and sustainable future not just for yourself but for humankind as well.

Imagine feeling better without medications that dull your sensibilities. Envision finding clarity that allows you to bring people together on issues no matter their stance. Visualize developing lasting love built on foundations of acceptance and transparency. Greater still, picture a reality where individuals know how to use their core instincts to be personally responsible and collectively peaceful, creating a fair, balanced and environmentally friendly planet. Intuition is the solution but it all starts with you.

HOW TO USE THIS BOOK

"Intuition is the source of scientific knowledge."

– Aristotle, Greek philosopher [iv]

THERE IS A SIMPLE science to how your intuition aids you in establishing personal well-being and collective harmony. You didn't learn this vital discipline in school, but you can easily gain knowledge of it and become proficient at it now. The information contained in this book serves as your intuitive manual, teaching you how to master your intuition, so that you experience improved health, establish deeper connections and have greater influence in shaping a healthier world.

Within this book, you will find a unique set of intuitive understandings. I developed these guidelines to help students gain quick access to their intuition while feeling safe and in control when exploring their inner senses. Additionally, you will find a plethora of stories, explanations, exercises and ethics designed to help you hone your higher senses. Funny thing, though – you can read about your intuition all day, but you will never know what it really can do until you experience it for yourself.

As great as this book is in providing you with supporting documentation on the use of your intuition, don't get so hung up on the science or ideals that you don't engage in the intuitive explorations. Let this book be more about the experience first, and then you can go back and reassess the theories to determine or refine your personal beliefs. Below is a summary of what you will find in each section of *Intuitively You*:

- Part I – Intuitive Understandings – In this section, you will find a unique set of guidelines for knowing and using your intuition. These guidelines will help you feel comfortable with the process of exploring your intuition, while also making you the authority of your experiences.

- Part II – Intuitively Aware – This part investigates your four cornerstone instincts. These senses will aid you in finding higher perspectives that allow you to feel confident in making your life choices. These foundations will also provide you with innovative ways of relating to others so you are promoting higher understanding and peaceful interactions with all.

- Part III – Intuitively Responsible – In this section, you will use your intuition to take charge of your fundamental energetics so that you can maintain optimal energy levels. As you assume higher command of your individual dynamics, you recognize every person's right to live their unique expression, initiating equality and harmony in the world.

- Part IV – Intuitively You – In this segment, you will learn to use your intuition to survey your four vital life foundations that will allow you to maintain a healthy environment physically, mentally, emotionally and spiritually. As you balance your primary life systems, you learn the secrets to transforming some of our culture's toughest issues such as healthcare, education, politics and religion, allowing people to find common ground.

- Part V – Intuitively United – This section takes your intuition to its next level. Here you will use your higher knowledge to explore your soul's history. From there, you will learn to bring greater awareness and healing to yourself, your family, your sense of purpose, and even your intimate relationship space. As you live intuitively in your everyday life, you offer the people around you the opportunity to transform their circumstances, evolving humankind.

- Part VI – Intuitively Ethical – Here you will discover a distinctive set of moral parameters for being intuitive in your everyday reality. These ethics will foster your ability to apply your inner knowledge in all areas of life in ways that promote transparency, acceptance and world peace.

- Additionally – In each chapter, you will find intuitive explorations, contemplative questions and transformative ways to evolve your thinking, so you can create the type of lifestyle that benefits you and the entire planet.

It is best to start at the beginning and work through the book systematically. The concepts in this text build on one another. You will want the foundational understanding of each section in order to support the stages of your growth throughout this exploration. As you read the chapters, test out the concepts in your everyday life to gauge their powers, referring back to the exercises whenever needed.

Let's begin your intuitive exploration now.

INTUITIVE UNDERSTANDINGS

Know How Intuition Works and Unlock Your Greatest Potential

"If you want to find the secrets of the universe, think in terms of energy, frequency and vibration."

– Nikola Tesla, Inventor

TRAINING INTUITIVES IS one of the best parts of my job. However, if it wasn't for a dear friend who insisted that I start an intuitive development class, I would never have entered the teaching arena. In fact, instructing others was the last thing I ever thought I'd be doing.

I'm dyslexic and consequently was undervalued in my early traditional schooling, being labeled a slow reader and someone who should never calculate numbers. However, I've come to know that just because my early education didn't recognize my unique way of receiving and processing information didn't mean I wasn't intelligent. Still I was torn. Who was I to think I could, or even should, teach others? I didn't want to inadvertently mislead someone or cause them harm in any way. (One of the first feelings you have as an intuitive is the sense to do no harm.) Yet if I were to honor my clients' needs by stepping into my teaching role, I would have to overcome my childhood programming, trusting that intuition would lead the way.

Drawing on my internal wisdom and with a no-guarantee clause, I began instructing everyday people how to use their intuitive powers. Fifteen years and multitudes of students later, I feel confident saying that I love teaching and find it to be one of my greatest strengths. More importantly, during my years of instructing, I developed an exceptionally quick and highly efficient system of helping students learn to function intuitively within a matter of minutes, contrary to the prolonged ways in which I learned.

When I attended clairvoyant school, I took six weeks of precursory courses just to establish the foundations for advancing into the twelve-month basic program. While I never perceived the pace of the curriculum as slow, when I began teaching intuitives, it became clear that I would need to pick up the pace.

With our busy lives today, most people don't have time for lengthy processes and need to be able to flip a switch that allows them to instantly access their higher awareness. As a result, I developed a series of seven guidelines for exploring intuition safely and effectively. Students, regardless of their knowledge base, can read and apply these concepts immediately in any intuitive development class, allowing them to begin finding solutions to their life's issues without delay. This allows students at varying levels of awareness to study and learn together, which, in my opinion, lends to more profound understandings and to the expansion of the whole. New intuitives receive the benefit of learning from advanced perspectives, seasoned intuitives receive the value of ingraining the basics, and both groups benefit from the ability to cut to the chase and delve into their life issues to find healing, empowerment and change.

Following are my straightforward understandings for how to approach your intuitive explorations in an easy and safe fashion. These understandings serve to minimize your fears and uncertainties about yourself and the process of exploring intuition so that you can jump into the practices without inadvertently creating blocks as you go through the book.

Intuitive Understanding # 1 - You are an Energetic Charge

Albert Einstein's pioneering theory of relativity shows us that everything is energy, and energy never ceases to exist – it simply changes form. What does this mean to you? You are energy too, and as such, you can change form at will, should you know how to use the full power of your higher mind. To understand better this concept of energy and its effects on your reality, read what scientist Lynne McTaggart discovered in her research on energy, intention and manifestation.

> *"Discoveries are being made that prove what religion has always espoused: human beings are far more extraordinary than an assemblage of flesh and bones. At its most fundamental, this new science answers questions that have perplexed scientists for hundreds of years. At its most profound this is a science of the miraculous…these studies offer us copious information about the central organizing force governing our bodies and the rest of the cosmos…we are not a chemical reaction, but an energetic charge. Human beings and all living things are a coalescence of energy in a field of energy connected to every other thing in the world…We are attached and engaged, indivisible from our world and our only fundamental truth is our relationship with it."* v

> Lynne McTaggart, *The Field*, from her epilogue "The Coming Revolution"

The above quote is profound. Lynne McTaggart is a leading researcher in the field of consciousness and its quantum effects. In her book *The Field*, she speaks of the scientific revolution of quantum consciousness, where we use our higher minds to direct the energetic universe to achieve personal health, peace and fulfillment. However, when I first read McTaggart's epilogue, I had to review it many times before I understood all its nuances. How could her findings apply to me, an individual leading an everyday life as a mother, entrepreneur, and woman trying to maintain her health and relationships? It all finally clicked for me when I understood one point that was not only important but life changing.

"... we are not a chemical reaction, but an energetic charge."

McTaggart notes that science once believed that life began due to a chemical reaction, implying that you are a result of chemistry with no control over your life process. Today, however, quantum science tells us that we are not a chemical reaction but an energetic charge, and it's our intentions that spark reality, which changes everything. As a chemical reaction, you are victim to circumstances. As an energetic charge, your intentions create your circumstances. Can you see the difference and the benefit? As a victim, you have no influence. As a charge, you are a creator with the power to shift course. Suddenly, life becomes anything you choose.

In that sense, McTaggart's words showed me that if I wanted to energetically shift my perspective away from being a victim to my upbringing, career and relationships, and assume responsibility as the creator of my life's circumstances, I could change my beliefs about myself and begin generating greater experiences in alignment with my higher ideals.

Don't be fooled into thinking that just because you cannot physically see energy that it's not important. You are pure energy before you are anything else. With a simple intuitive prompting, you can direct the flow of energy in any way you wish. Try the exercise below to become familiar with the etheric forces of potential within you and all around you.

Feel Energy

Start by vigorously rubbing your hands together to activate and clear the energy centers located in your palms. Next, place your palms together and then slowly draw them apart. Let your hands feel, or sense, the energy in the space in between. Play with the energy by moving your hands closer together and then farther apart, noticing the subtle differences at certain distances.

Once you have an understanding of what your personal energy feels like, place your hand(s) over a plant, or any object, and sense how its energy differs from your own. Recognize that all things, living and inanimate, have an energetic signature, however subtle it may be. The more you hone your intuition, the better you become at sensing the nuances between these signatures and their symbolic meanings.

Continue to practice playfully feeling the energy of the people and items around you as a means of gaining greater awareness of the etheric world.

Intuitive Understanding # 2 - Your Thoughts Spark Your Reality

As I mentioned a moment ago, an intuitive suggestion can direct the flow of energy in any way you wish. To support this notion, an experiment known as Hardy's Paradox describes just how energy is influenced by thought.

> *"In a quantum state, photons that are observed change their attributes; for intention is the observation to create change. Without intent, nothing happens."*[vi]

This scientific finding demonstrates that your intentions, or thoughts, serve as the central organizing force that creates movement in the energetic field, thereby coalescing energy into density and form. Simply put, your thoughts manifest your reality. When you command energy to move, it moves.

To support Hardy's Paradox further, scientist Dr. Masaru Emoto's conscious experiments with water [vii] overwhelmingly demonstrate how water's crystalline structures transform when the person observing the water changes his or her feelings. For example, when the observer's thoughts were of love and peace, beautiful and complex geometric crystalline structures formed in the water. At the same time, intentions such as hate and fear created grotesque and ill-formed blobs of unhealthy crystalline masses. This is important because you, being mostly water, are your inner viewpoints and have more control over your reality than you know. However, your mind's projections can be an unruly bunch. It is widely theorized that people have roughly 70,000 thoughts a day.[viii] This is why changing behaviors can be difficult. Of course, the trick becomes using your intuition to isolate as well as interpret which internal dialogues create the life you desire and which hinder your circumstances.

Your thoughts repeat, and in that sense, they ingrain energy into patterns of belief. A repetitive thought of "I love myself " creates a healthy pattern, leading to a lifetime of connection and empowerment. At the same time, a repetitive thought such as "I'm not good enough" creates unhealthy perceptions that lead to depression and isolation. Throughout this book, I will provide you with innovative ways of thinking that will shift your mental projections so that you are creating from your highest and greatest good.

Intuitive Understanding # 3 - Intuition Offers Solutions and Opportunities

Your intuition exists for two primary reasons. First, intuition facilitates access to and communication with universal wisdom. This connection to higher knowledge allows you to find innovative solutions to your personal issues so that you can thrive in all areas and phases of your life.

Second, your intuition aids you in accessing universal potential – the place where all new opportunities exist awaiting your recognition so that they can be brought into reality for the betterment of the world.

Your job is to pay attention to what the universe is communicating, either about your personal issues, or about solutions that benefit all.

Intuitive Understanding # 4 - Symbolism is the Language of the Universe

Now familiarize yourself with the way energy grabs your intuition's attention. Energy speaks to you in the form of symbols, which is thought to be a universal language. Energy shapes itself into symbolic images, frequencies, sensations, and vibrations as a way of communicating with you. You receive these messages based on your personal frame of reference.

What I mean is that a sign only equates what you determine it means. For instance, if your intuition perceives the color sky-blue in regards to your mental health, you might interpret that to mean peace and calm. At the same time, if I were to intuit sky-blue for my mental health, I might find it to mean loftiness and disconnect. Do you see my point?

Everyone interprets symbolism differently based on his or her unique experiences and beliefs. Therefore, your interpretation is always correct and is ultimately the only one that matters. Yet I would caution that not every symbol or sign you receive means something profound. Oftentimes when you start an intuitive journey, you will notice many odd coincidences or synchronicities and wonder what the universe is trying to tell you. People report finding feathers in odd places, pennies everywhere they go or disembodied spirits around them, but don't know why and worry that they're missing a message from the universe. However, these events are mostly happening to make you pay more attention to your intuition, not to bring you the next winning lottery numbers. As you begin your intuitive discovery, pay attention to the symbolism in your everyday life so that you begin to master its language.

One of my favorite ways of honing my symbolic language is to notice the interesting occurrences happening around me, and then researching what the metaphor might imply. For instance, I once experienced a span of two weeks in which foxes would suddenly show up at the craziest times and places. I figured it was too big to be a coincidence and must have a bigger message for me. I then searched the internet to find what others thought the symbol of the fox represented to see if it resonated with something occurring in my life.

Curiously, one of the fox's traits is adaptability. Immediately upon reading that, I felt a sense of truth ring within me. At the time, the building I was officing in was being sold. I was comfortable there and didn't like the idea of finding a new space. However, I felt that the fox was telling me to be adaptable and accepting of change. Heeding the message, I warmed up to the idea of moving. Interestingly, it wasn't long before I found an office that could offer me more than my previous location – something I hadn't thought possible.

I've often wondered: If I had continued to be resistant to a move, would I have found the better situation? I'm glad I'll never know. As part of your intuitive understandings, and as one of the elements to enhance your empowerment, learn to interpret symbolism. Notice what is happening around you, and begin to decode your life's events so that you can find solutions to your everyday circumstances.

Intuitive Understanding # 5 - You Cannot Use Intuition Incorrectly

Of these understandings, this concept is my favorite. Why? Because intuitive perception is unique to every person, and therefore you cannot do it wrong. In whatever way the intuitive process works for you, it's correct! Don't let anyone make you feel bad because you don't experience your intuition their way. Find contentment in how the process works for you individually.

However, note that it's not your intuition's job to make your life perfect. I know… if only. I think it's worth recognizing that your core instincts will at times lead you into experiences that are difficult or may seem wrong. If I only had the proverbial dime for every time a client said to me, "I don't know what when wrong; I thought he was my soulmate," I'd own an island. Just remember, you likely need those heartbreaking moments for your personal growth. Try not to blame your intuition. Rather use it to understand the lesson it is leading you to discover so that you can find greater healing and life expansion.

Also, as you develop your intuition, you will experience times when you feel it's operating at full capacity and times when you wonder if it's working at all. Keep following these techniques and exercises, and you will discover that there is a flow to when your intuition heightens versus when it dulls.

Intuitive Understanding # 6 - Imagination's Role in Developing Intuition

Interestingly, I find this understanding to be the most needed. I often hear people just beginning their intuitive development say that they feel their imaginations are making up what their core instincts are sensing. This feeling of fantasy makes it difficult for them to trust their instincts. However, imagination serves both the intellect and the intuition. It should be a part of the intuitive process.

Imagination allows you to define a symbol as well as receive a symbol. Let's say you are imagining yourself playing with a beach ball on the Caribbean sands. In that moment, you are using your imagination to direct the universe, giving it a symbolic command: "I want to go to the beach." However, if you look beyond what you defined, suddenly your imagination is receiving a symbolic message back from the universe about how to achieve your ideals.

For instance, if you revisit your beach scene and look to see what is happening that you didn't intend, you might unexpectedly see your partner sipping margaritas by the shore, indicating that he or she is open to a sun-filled vacation when perhaps you thought differently.

The point is that imagination is the bridge between intellect and intuition. You can use imagination to direct or receive an image, as that is its function. While you explore interpreting your intuitive symbols, it's perfectly acceptable not to deny your imagination but let it be a part of the process, as it can show you what you didn't know, as well as confirm what you may have expected.

Intuitive Understanding # 7 - Use All Four of Your Cornerstone Instincts

Lastly, you will want to consider the four cornerstones by which your intuition operates. While your traditional five senses relate to the physical world, you have four cornerstone instincts that allow you to see, hear, feel and know what is taking place within the energetic reality. It's important that you develop and learn to rely on all your intuitive cornerstones, as this ultimately makes you a well-rounded individual. You will explore and become familiar with these four foundations next.

Armed with these seven intuitive understandings, you can feel safe, confident, and in control of your intuitive development. Apply these guidelines as you move through the information and exercises in this book, and refer back to them as needed.

PART II

INTUITIVELY AWARE

Use Higher Perspective to Discover Personal and Global Peace

"As my awareness increases, my control over my own being increases."

– William Schutz, American Psychologist [ix]

IRIS NEEDED A fresh start and wanted to move out of state. While Iris was positive that moving was her next adventure, she was indecisive about where to go. She had been contemplating two locations but was unsure which best supported her aspirations and sought my insight for clarity.

My session with Iris was extensive. I helped her understand what the essence of each place would create as experience for her and how each would assist in her growth. When we finished, Iris said she felt calmer, and more importantly, she felt certain which of the two states was best for her. She was ready to move the minute she left my office. However, as part of the ethics of being intuitive, I suggested that Iris not take my word for it or make sudden decisions based on what I interpreted. Rather, she should allow her intuition to validate whether or not her choice was sound.

I instructed Iris to take the next week to pay extra attention to her inner senses to see what they might reveal about relocating. Over the week, Iris was to notice what inner impressions, picture, thoughts and feelings she was having, as well as paying attention to the conversations and synchronicities happening around her. By being intuitively aware, she could receive the messages that would serve to confirm or contradict her choice.

Iris followed my advice. During her week of heightened intuitive awareness, she overhead a couple talking about their fabulous vacation to the state she was considering. Iris also talked about hearing a song repeating in her head that she vaguely remembered but didn't know. When she looked up the lyrics, she found the name of the state buried in a verse. However, Iris said she was sure she was on her proper path when suddenly she had a vision of herself driving a different direction to work. She turned quickly to accommodate her inner prompting and found herself behind a car with a license place from the state in which she now resides.

You are always, and always have been, receiving intuitive information guiding you toward the answers to your questions. When you don't know how to attune to those messages, it is easy to get off track and become lost in your life. If you are uncertain about your job, a love interest or even your health, using intuitive awareness will lead you to your answers.

Interestingly, in the 1970s and 80s, the CIA in conjunction with the Stanford Research Institute began conducting experiments meant to prove or disprove psychic abilities.[x] Much to their surprise, the researchers not only confirmed that extrasensory faculties exist, but they also mastered those skills and built systems, such as Remote Viewing, to provide protocols for increasing their otherworldly accuracy.

One of the original researchers, Dr. Russell Targ, wrote an article in 2015 entitled "The Reality of ESP: A Physicist's Proof of Psychic Abilities."[xi] Referencing his forty years of psychic research, he stated, "Based on all these decades of data, I believe it would be logically unreasonable to deny the reality of some kind of human ability for direct awareness or experience of distant events that are blocked from ordinary perception." Targ goes on to say, "In my experience and according to most other researchers, it appears that an experienced psychic can answer any question that has an answer. I cannot wait to see what the future holds when we fully open the doors of our perception! It is time to accept the gift of psychic abilities. The hardware is fine; it's the software that must be upgraded — and quickly."

And quickly!

Your intuitive knowledge is needed now more than ever. If we are going to think our way out of the world's problems, upgrading your software by accessing higher perception is where to find the answers.

Below is a description of your four cornerstone instincts. These core senses will aid you in shifting perspectives so that you can find your higher solutions to evolving your personal circumstances as well as ways of transitioning our cultural beliefs away from indifference and separation toward understanding and acceptance.

1. Clairvoyance (Clear Seeing): Clairvoyance allows you to see and project symbolic images and stories in your mind's eye, giving you information about your health, wealth and wellbeing. Your higher sight also allows you to see another person's perspective in ways that promote harmony within all your relationships, enlightening the world around you.

2. Clairaudience (Clear Hearing): Clairaudience allows you to hear words and detect frequency vibrations that tell you the nature of your circumstances and how best to stay on your personal path. Your higher attunement also aids you in becoming a better listener so that you are engaged in your relationships, creating common ground and diplomacy with all people.

3. Clairsentience (Clear Sensing): Clairsentience allows you to feel emotions, taste auras, and even sense the pain of others so that you become aware of the factors influencing your life and can change them at will. Your heightened feelings also provide you with the ability to connect deeply to other people, initiating empathy that promotes balanced partnerships and caring communities.

4. Claircognizance (Clear Knowing): Claircognizance relates directly to your ability to know something with absolute truth and provides

you with the power to live your most authentic life. Your knowingness is also instrumental in accessing innovative global ideas with the potential to reinvent our harried daily routines, stabilize earth's climate and even create world peace.

While your core instincts have always been working, you may not have been aware of them or taken them seriously as a guidance system or means of finding the meaning in your circumstances so you can transform your life. In this section, you will learn to use your fundamental intuitive senses to discover new ways of relating to yourself and others.

CLAIRVOYANCE
The Intuitive Act of Clear Seeing

"Close both eyes to see with the other."

– Rumi, Poet

ONCE DURING A meditation, Mia had a vision flash in her mind's eye of a red vehicle crashing into her while she was driving her car. The impression was so unexpected that Mia could no longer concentrate and ended her meditation with the feeling that she was in imminent doom. Needless to say, she was on guard.

Over the next several weeks, Mia remained alert to every red car near her. Then one day as she was driving down a busy road, she noticed a large red SUV pulling out of a neighborhood. She could see that the woman driving didn't notice her, as the woman was rapidly advancing into the intersection. Mia immediately slowed down and in her head yelled to the driver, "Don't you see me?" The woman suddenly did a double take, as if receiving the telepathic thought, and slammed on her breaks to avoid the potential accident. Mia's heart leaped with relief. What might have happened in that moment if she hadn't taken her clairvoyant prompting seriously and been on the lookout for trouble?

This happened to my sister once. She was leaving work one evening and had an image flash in her mind of getting into a car accident on her way home. Sadly, she didn't validate her instinct by taking a different route and instead went about her regular commute. Sure enough, in the exact intersection she had envisioned, an uninsured driver ran a red light and hit her. Although my sister didn't suffer a severe injury from the incident, she was shaken by the fact that her intuition had given her a warning meant to keep her completely safe, but she hadn't listened. Instead, she spent the next several months depleting her time and resources to repair her car and rehabilitate her body. My sister now takes every intuitive prompting seriously.

Do you have a vivid imagination or dreams full of color, detail and life? Can you recall a time when you had a vision of something that later happened? It's more than likely that you ignored those images, having no idea that your higher sight was sending you vital information. Let's explore your clairvoyance now so that you can learn how to use your intuitive ability to see clearly with confidence and certainty.

Explore Your Clairvoyance

Clairvoyance means clear-seeing and is the intuitive ability that allows you to witness images, impressions and subtle energies for the purpose of interpreting their symbolism. Any time you see an image in your mind's eye, your inner sight is sending you a message. People who frequently daydream or have lively imaginations are highly clairvoyant and are often instrumental in bringing new ideas to the collective, such as Nikola Telsa, Leonardo da Vinci and even Steve Jobs.

The following exercise will help you explore your ability to see energy. The purpose of this exploration is to introduce you to your intuition's ability to witness symbolic impressions as well as to let you know how much development this skill requires. In chapter three, you will start using your higher senses to create personal and collective change. For now, simply become familiar with how your intuitive senses operate so that you can begin to rely on them with greater confidence.

1. Begin by closing your eyes. This will help you attune to your inner images more clearly.
2. Next, imagine a tree in front of you. You don't have to know anything about trees. Simply take a moment and use your clear-seeing ability to allow your imagination to show you a tree.
3. Take note of the tree's size and shape as well as where it is in its growth cycle. Is the tree in a forest, park or off the street? Is it day or night, summer or winter? Observe the scene, gleaning as much detail as possible.

When you have finished your exploration, take a moment to journal or contemplate how well this faculty is operating for you. Ask yourself the following questions:

- How easy or difficult was it to see my tree and why?
- What was the quality of my imagery – crisp, vibrant, blurred or foggy?
- What might this tree tell me about the state of my health, relationships, purpose, etc.?
- Do I feel my clairvoyance needs honing, or is it operating optimally?
- How could this skill be useful in my life?

Develop Your Clairvoyance

Clairvoyance was not my strongest intuitive ability. However, I found it very easy to develop. In an effort to train myself to see more, I started to pay extra attention to the images that would float through my mind like daydreams, and it worked. Within a few months, I was seeing energy with greater detail. Now, fifteen years of intuitive work later, clairvoyance is one of my favorite, strongest and most reliable aptitudes. I often say that my job is like going to the movies. I watch my clients' tales unfold, finding the moral of their stories that will help them move beyond negative patterns and beliefs.

As you gain an understanding of how your clairvoyance operates, you will want to develop and sustain this part of yourself. However, if you find that your higher sight is strong enough or that it's overwhelming you, don't feel the need to expand it at this time. Focus on developing your other senses to find a greater balance. Otherwise, here are a few ways you can increase your clairvoyance so that it becomes a more reliable asset in your life:

1. If you think about it, you often see pictures in your mind's eye very naturally. One of the best ways to develop your clairvoyance is by paying attention to the images and scenes that flash before you as you go about your day. When you are speaking with others, stopped at a red light, reading a book, working with colleagues, etc., give extra attention to the images playing in your mind. You may even want to keep a journal on hand to take special note of the images you see throughout the day so that you can revisit the impressions to gain greater clarity.

2. Another great way to develop your clairvoyance is by recalling your dreams and focusing on their details. Everyone has experienced a time when they've had a vivid dream. Bring that vision back into your consciousness, and spend time surveying the scene, recalling as much detail as possible. This practice will heighten the clarity of your inner sight.

3. You may be aware of the concept of visualization but might not know how it works. Visualization is a highly concentrated form of thought that is specifically great at magnetizing your reality to you quickly. The effectiveness of using higher intentions to manifest tangible results is why this technique is another wonderful way to develop your clairvoyance. Try making a habit of being still and envisioning the life you desire. This not only enhances your ability to see, but it also aids you in consciously creating your ideal reality.

Evolve Your Thinking

To follow up your clairvoyant exploration and development, it will be necessary to notice your inner dialogue to discover the beliefs you have about your ability to see energy. If you recall, you have roughly 70,000 thoughts a day that are responsible for creating your reality. You will want to isolate the thoughts that reflect negative ideals, such as these, "I can't see energy," "There is no such thing as clairvoyance," or "I don't have the right to see what is in my best interest." Shift these messages so that you can heighten your clairvoyance.

I've provided some alternative phrases you can substitute for your negative chatter. Use these sayings like mantras, repeating the expressions until they become your new beliefs. However, you don't have to use my words. Feel free to create thoughts to match your unique circumstances. Here are some examples:

"I have every right to see clearly and determine what is in my best interest."

"Visualizing is fun and a great way to design my ideal life."

"Everyone is clairvoyant, including me!"

Clairvoyance Promotes Peace by Seeing Other People's Points of View

Fifteen years ago, I hosted a talk-radio show discussing the topic of intuition. However, after my first episode, the board of directors considered canceling my program. It seemed that one of the board members had taken offense to my subject matter. Worse still, I would have to endure this director's wrath, as she saw fit to use her position to bully me in hopes that I would leave the station.

It began when I was asked to attend a meeting where for twenty minutes, I listened to one of the female directors tell me I was a conniving charlatan who had nothing to offer society. She not only demeaned my knowledge but questioned my character and right to free expression. To say the least, I was shocked and hurt. I found myself growing increasingly angry with each droplet of spittle that flew from her unyielding mouth. I was so mad, in fact, that my heart began racing, and my stomach tied into knots. No longer listening to her rhetoric, I began plotting my ultra-fervent quantum-scientific defense. After all, I simply couldn't understand why she was so hell bent on tearing me down. But then suddenly the situation took a very unexpected turn.

Out of the blue, I intuitively received a picture of myself opening my energetic heart-center and sending the board member a stream of unconditional love. Wanting to annihilate her more than love her, I tried to push the image aside, but it wouldn't leave my mind's eye. Yet, as my heart palpitations worsened, I figured it couldn't hurt to offer higher energy to the situation. As the vision instructed, I opened my heart, sending the director all the positive energy I could muster. While it didn't stop her rant, it did calm my frustration, which, in the long run, was the key to resolving our difference.

As I calmed myself, I was able to focus on another clairvoyant picture presenting itself, this time of the woman. I saw her as a small child, alone and fearful of a world she knew little about. Immediately I felt sympathy for my bully. She seemed lonely, and I imagined that her volunteer efforts at the station were the only place she received any real human interaction and acknowledgement. I realized that she just needed her opinions heard, regardless of what anyone thought about it, including me. Understanding that the woman was belittling me due to her own sense of fear and lack of connection, when it came time for me to defend myself, I was no longer angry; I was empathetic.

When the board of directors asked me how I'd like to respond to the matter, I calmly stated, "It seems I need to be more educational with my content." Much to my surprise, that's all I had to say. The board quickly agreed and concluded the meeting. Interestingly, the board seemed bothered that they'd had to take time out of their busy schedules for what amounted to a non-issue. It made me feel as if it wasn't the first time my bully had needlessly caused a drama for the sake of getting attention. However, I'm sure the board was used to much more animosity from others under those circumstances. They appeared appreciative of my calm reaction. In a sense, clairvoyance served as my superpower, quelling what could have been a potentially explosive situation, bringing a natural and peaceful resolution to the conflict.

Part of the shifts in thinking we are noticing today can be seen in the trend toward superheros in film and television. For the last two decades, superheroes have blockbusted onto not only the big screen but also into our homes in the form of action figures and logoed merchandise. But why would we revere people with seemingly impossible powers? Because, deep inside our intuitions are telling us that we are more than we appear to be and that we have the ability to transform the lives of humanity for the better.

Clairvoyance is one of your four cornerstone instincts that provides you with superhero capabilities and the means to create harmony in the world. Your inner sight offers you perspective so that you can understand another person's point of view regardless of his or her stance, allowing you to reach mutual understandings.

The more you pay attention to your inner sight, the more adept you become at being aware of your personal motivations, the intention of others, and life's greater truths. Begin using this superpower in your everyday life in order to heighten your own reality and contributing to the betterment of all.

CLAIRAUDIENCE
The Intuitive Act of Clear Hearing

"To whatever degree you listen and follow your intuition, you become a creative channel for the higher power of the universe."

– Shakti Gawain, Author

ONE MORNING WHILE getting ready for work, I heard the lyrics to the 1980s song, "I Can't Drive 55" by Sammy Hagar repeating in my head. To be honest, I've never really been a fan of that song or music genre, yet for some reason, I quickly began to unconsciously sing the tune. However, because I was busily preparing for my day, I didn't even notice the melody repeating in the background of my mind. It wasn't until I grabbed my keys and was leaving home that I suddenly realized I had been playing the tune on a loop in my head all morning. But why?

I stopped and consciously asked myself what message the lyrics had for me. Immediately, I remembered that my fourteen-year-old Subaru Outback was on her last wheel. The car was experiencing several issues that even my mechanic felt weren't worth fixing. I knew the song was telling me that the vehicle I had loved and owned for far too long could literally not drive 55 anymore. Heeding the message, I bought a new car that day.

Have you ever noticed recurring thoughts, lyrics and ideas passing through your mind? Are you sensitive to sound and loud noises? It's easy to dismiss something of this nature, never knowing that your clairaudience is at work, bringing you the pieces to your life's puzzle.

Explore Your Clairaudience

Clairaudience means clear hearing and is the intuitive ability that allows you to hear energetic frequencies, resonances and vibrations describing the nature of something. Whenever you hear a ringing in your ears, your inner voice speaking to you, or the voice of another not physically present, your clairaudience is involved. Musicians are naturally clairaudient, as they often hear a melody in their head before composing it on paper. Go ahead and explore your clairaudience by following the intuitive practice you find here. The purpose of this exercise is to notice how clearly you hear frequency, tone and vibration and to find out if this skill needs development.

1. Start by quieting your mind and closing your eyes.
2. Next, focus on all the sounds around you – the birds outside, the hum of the lights above you, the sound of cars passing nearby, even the frequency of the chair you are sitting in. Isolate each sound and give it individual attention.
3. Once you've listened intently to your environment, pay attention to your inner thoughts. What is your mind saying about this exercise and all that you are learning?
4. Now listen for the voice and thoughts of someone you know, like your mother, best friend, spouse, or child. Listen to what they have to say to you in this moment, whether it's about the process you are exploring or about life in general. Simply attune to their frequency, vibration, tone and message, discerning their sound from your own.

After completing the exercise, take a moment and consider how well this faculty is operating for you. Ask yourself the following questions:

- How many different sounds could I decipher?
- Could I hear my own voice speaking to me? What did it say and why?
- Could I hear the voice of someone familiar to me? Who was it? What did they have to say and how is their voice different from my own?
- What influence does this person have in my life?
- Is my clairaudient skill working well or do I need to develop it further?
- How can I use this skill in my everyday life?

Develop Your Clairaudience

When I started my intuitive education, clairaudience was my most developed skill. If you recall from the introduction, a clairaudient experience prompted my journey back to intuition. Today, as an intuitive practitioner, I prefer my clairaudient skill above all others, because I feel confident relying on it. When I'm in a therapy session with a client, I relay verbatim the information I receive, which is always profound and right on target with their needs and issues.

You can develop your clairaudience to very fine degrees. However, if you find this skill is operating at full capacity, focus on developing your other senses to find greater balance. If you'd like to develop this skill, the following is a set of intuitive practices you can use to hone and sustain your clairaudience so that you can depend on it as an asset in designing your ideal world.

1. One of the best ways to develop your clairaudience is to practice listening more and speaking less. Most people are not good listeners. Their minds race with what they want to say in response causing

unhealthy miscommunications. During your day, stop your mind from wandering. Focus on the moment. Listen to what others say without needing to respond unless requested.

2. Another great way to sustain your clairaudience is to notice the voices in your head. If that sounds crazy, it's really not that odd. To this day, I can still hear my 1st grade teacher saying to me, "That was an excellent use of your words," praising me for reprimanding a boy who wouldn't follow the rules. I'm sure you can hear in your head the words others have imparted to you as well. However, you may not have realized that your clairaudience was responsible for the recall. See if you can consciously pick out your voice from that of your family, partner, and friends. This will help you become familiar with the many vibrational nuances associated with clear hearing ability, as well as who may be having sway over your personal beliefs.

Evolve Your Thinking

You will also want to consider the thoughts you have about being clairaudient. It's necessary to isolate the limiting beliefs within you that sound something like this: "I can't hear energy," "There is no such thing as clairaudience," or "I don't deserve to hear what is in my best interest." Shift those thoughts into higher ideals. Use the suggestions below to change your inner dialogue, or get creative and design your own.

"Hearing energy makes me cool and interesting."

"I am free to hear the path that is best for me."

"The entire world exists of energy and frequency that I can hear and discern!"

Clairaudience Fosters Understanding and Acceptance for All

Leo was an exceptionally caring man who loved his wife Ginger, never wanting her to endure hardship of any kind. Consequently, each time Ginger voiced a stressful life concern, Leo would interrupt her, jumping into action and stopping her from expressing any negativity by proposing all the ways in which she could resolve her issue without being unhappy. The only problem was that Ginger wasn't asking her husband to fix her problems. Rather, Ginger needed to vent her frustrations mostly to hear herself so that she could determine her own best courses of actions. It bothered Ginger that her husband cut short those types of conversations. She respected his desire to make her life easy, but it made her feel as though her negative emotions were not acceptable and that she was only allowed to show one side of herself . . . . happy.

Yet, there is a strong need in women today to be heard. Ginger wanted Leo to listen more and instruct less. She wanted to feel comfortable being angry in a moment so that she could process her life events, grow from her experiences and then reestablish her joy. Unfortunately, as well meaning and genuine as Leo's love was, he was shutting off her full expression, causing a rift in their marriage.

Communication gaps like Ginger and Leo experienced happen to all of us in our relationships. The way to avoid these types of misunderstandings is to use your higher ability to hear clearly.

Clairaudience is another one of your intuition's superpowers designed to balance yourself and the world. Your ability to hear the perspectives of others clearly, without the need to respond or fix them, allows them to feel witnessed and received, which is all anyone really needs in order to be happy. With this knowledge, you can begin using your clairaudience in your daily routines, listening more than speaking, allowing acceptance to rule the world.

CLAIRSENTIENCE
The Intuitive Act of Clear Sensing

"Trust your gut feelings. That's where true wisdom manifests itself."

– Oprah Winfrey, Media Mogul and Philanthropist

BRITA HAD BEEN developing her core instincts for several months but was questioning how learning to use them was going to help her in her life. Then one day she received her answer. Brita was standing in line at a busy coffeehouse. Although the wait was long, Brita was excited to get a hot drink and immerse herself in a work assignment she had proudly been awarded. However, as Brita stood in line, she began to notice that she was feeling sad and that all her positive energy was draining away. It was subtle at first, but with each passing ring of the register, her agitation grew. In just minutes, the thought of sitting and working all day felt like drudgery.

This sudden mood swing seemed odd to Brita. How could she lose interest in her anticipated project so quickly when just moments before, she had been enthusiastic about completing her task? Thankfully, Brita remembered her intuitive training. While standing in line, Brita began to use her clairsentience to scan her environment and detect what was causing her shift in motivation. It was then that Brita realized she was reacting to the emotions of another person.

When Brita intuitively felt the energies of the space around her, she noticed the energy of a young girl around eleven who was sitting with her mother and her mother's friends. The women were busily chatting and catching up, and Brita could sense the young girl's resentment about having to sit with nothing to do while her mother and friends had all the fun.

Brita laughed at herself. She knew her clear-feeling sense was her strongest core instinct but had no idea how powerfully it influenced her. This episode helped Brita understand why most of her life, she had been so easily pulled off her personal path and why she was so often called overly emotional and moody. With this knowledge, Brita quickly used her intuitive tools to reset her space and send the girl's energy back to her. After regaining her sense of self, Brita then went about her productive day as planned.

Has something like what happened to Brita every happen to you? Can you recall a time when you walked into a room and immediately felt the emotions of the people or the setting? Because we are a culture that doesn't teach the science of subtle energy, most people get bombarded by the emotions of others, having no idea or control over how that can affect their personal reality. If you don't know how to discern your emotions from someone else's, you become a victim to circumstances that could potentially steer you off course.

Explore Your Clairsentience

Clairsentience means clear sensing and is the intuitive ability to feel emotions, sensations and even the taste of energy. When you resonate with another person's feelings, your clairsentience is at work. Introverts and empaths are naturally clairsentient, which is why they generally prefer isolation to social activity. It can be overwhelming to process all the energies around them, especially if they don't know how to manage their higher sensibilities; being reclusive seems to be the safest stance. However, learning to hone and manage your empathic self means you don't have to shy away from the world.

You can explore your clairsentience by following the intuitive practice you find here. The purpose of this exercise is to notice how clearly you feel energy and emotions and how much this skill requires development.

1. You can start by closing your eyes and becoming still. Now take a moment and use your clairsentience and simply feel the room around you.

2. With your eyes shut, notice the vibrations, frequencies and energy of the things surrounding you. Feel the vibration of the chair beneath you. Sense the frequency of the plants in the room. Feel the energy of the open space around you. Get a general sense for what the room feels like, and see if you can distinguish the individual items in the area.

3. Next, ask to have the essence of someone you trust come into your room, like a parent, child or friend. Notice how their energy feels and how it shifts the environment. Notice whether you can smell their perfume, cologne or body wash.

Once you have completed your exploration, journal or contemplate your experience. Ask yourself the following questions:

- How easy or difficult was it to feel my environment?
- Could I discern the different feelings of each object in the room? What did I notice?
- How did the room shift when I invited another person's energy into the space? How did that affect me?
- How operational is my clairsentience? Does it need honing?
- How can I use this skill in my everyday life?

Develop Your Clairsentience

Clairsentience was the toughest of the skills for me to master. Clear sensing requires being open to feeling emotions, something I was discouraged from as a child. Consequently, not being emotionally sensitive was causing my relationships to weaken and my heart to harden. Thankfully, as I practiced this skill, it prompted my heart to activate and my emotions to expand, some of the greatest gifts I've given myself. I'm now able to bond more deeply in my relationships while also maintaining love for myself.

While you gain a greater understanding of how your clear sensing operates, you can develop this skill to enhance its capabilities. However, many intuitives are overly clairsentient, becoming consumed by other people's emotions to the detriment of their health, time and resources. If that is the case for you, don't expand this skill further. When you get to the section in this book on boundaries, you will want to make that intuitive practice a priority, as they will protect you from energy. For now, follow the practices below to expand your emotional capacity if needed.

1. The best starting place for developing your empathic skills is to become highly aware of your personal emotions. As you go about a day, chart how you feel first thing in the morning and as the day moves along. Notice when your emotions shift, and chart the difference. For example:

    - 8:00 am Feeling excited for the day.
    - 10:30 am Received phone call that deflated my energy.
    - 4:50 pm Was told I could leave early and feel thrilled.
    - 7:00 pm With my sweetie and feeling loved.
    - 9:15 pm Relief, finally sitting down to do nothing and feel nothing.

    The point is to become aware of the many feelings you traverse in a day and to notice how that affects your reality.

2. You can also develop your clairsentience by becoming aware of the emotions taking place around you, like Brita did in the coffeehouse. Whether you are at work, with family or even alone watching television, use your clairsentience to feel the emotions floating through the ether. Just be sure not to take on the emotions of others as if they are your own.

Evolve Your Thinking

Now you will want to observe the thoughts and beliefs you have about being clairsentient. Find the thoughts within you that resemble these: "You cannot feel energy," "There is no such thing as clairsentience," or "I don't have the right to feel what is in my best interest." Change any negative beliefs to something supportive that will adhere to your higher sense of self. Of course, you can use the following higher phrases I've provided or devise your own.

"My feelings are worthy and keep me safe."

"I don't have to take on the feelings of others."

"Feeling my way through life empowers me."

Clairsentience Generates Compassion Among Humankind

I was once at the airport during an exceptionally high travel period. The ticket lines were spilling over with passengers hoping to make their flights. Worse still were the trains to the terminals. Hoards of individuals stood poised, ready to pour themselves into the trolleys. There were so many people in fact that a businessman, a woman with two children, and I had already missed two trains due to overcrowding and being pushed aside. Frustrated, we collectively decided to press forward regardless of whom or what got in our way. When the next train arrived, we began our advancement. The competition was stiff as we pushed ourselves toward the train car, but unwilling to yield, we finally made our way on board. However, just as the train door was closing, the businessman spied an elderly woman trying desperately to embark. Restraining the gate with his back, he pulled the woman into the coach and then quickly exited, giving her his spot. As the doors shut, he smiled at us. I couldn't help but feel as though the business man resonated with our plights and wanted to ensure that us women were safely on our way.

One of our largest shifts taking place today is our ability to empathize with others. Clairsentience is another one of your intuition's healing cornerstones and subsequent superpowers. Clairsentience connects us all, invoking our consideration for one another by putting us in each other's shoes so we can find common ground. It is in our higher ability to truly *feel* for one another that we can learn to live together harmoniously. You can now take this knowledge and apply it to your everyday circumstances, allowing compassion to change the world.

CLAIRCOGNIZANCE
The Intuitive Act of Clear Knowing

"When we consistently suppress and distrust our intuitive knowingness, looking instead for authority, validation, and approval from others, we give our personal power away."

– Shakti Gawain, Author

BEING A HOCKEY mom to my three sons was one of the greatest joys of my life. However, it was also one of the most time-consuming sacrifices I have ever lent my efforts toward. At the first parent hockey meeting I attended, it was clear that this sport would require our utmost commitment. While I didn't necessarily subscribe to that theory, the trade-off was that my boys were learning life skills of teamwork, leadership, dedication and how to follow a passion . . . not to mention, I would always know where they could be found . . . on the ice.

After well over a decade of attending every game, I decided I deserved a break and stopped going to all the competitions when my youngest son was playing his last year of club hockey in college. In fact, not having children at home meant that I could focus more on my career. I was writing my first book then, rather than cheering in the stands. Still, I knew the hockey schedule and would attend on occasion.

Though I hadn't been in a while, one day I felt the need to be at a game. Unfortunately, I was also finishing my book and didn't want to stop my creative flow. As I internally debated between my responsibilities, I had a terrible knowingness that my baby was going to be injured. However, I pushed the sense aside, thinking I was being irrational and feeling guilty for not attending. In the end, I chose to complete my work despite my nagging sense that at any moment I was going to get a call confirming my worst fears. That call never came.

Oddly, the next morning I still felt my sense of impending doom, so I reached out to my son to inquire about his evening. Immediately I could tell something was off by the way he groggily muttered his hello to me. He then said, "Mom, you'll never believe what happened. I shattered my ankle in the game last night." There it was . . . my intuition confirmed! I had known that my son was going to get hurt. I don't know why he didn't call me immediately afterward but some issues can't be solved with intuition. However, I also realized that even if I had been at the rink, I wouldn't have been able to prevent the accident. I don't mind saying that I'm glad I didn't see it, but maybe that's the point.

You cannot prevent another person's negative circumstances, because they are meant to grow from those events. The truth is that my son was reaching his end with hockey. He felt it was taking too much time away from his studies and the other areas of life he wanted to explore. However, growing up with a sense of brotherhood and commitment, he didn't want to let his team down and allowed them to convince him to playing another season when he likely should have opted out. Thankfully, my son's injury provided the excuse he needed to move forward in his life. I can't help but wonder if the reason I elected not to attend the game was because my higher self knew the incident would be unpreventable, and it would be best if I didn't witness my son's initial trauma.

Can you remember a time when you knew something was going to happen and then it did? Have you ever had an unspoken thought in your head, only to have the person you are with say what you were thinking? We generally think of these odd events as insignificant, never realizing that our inner knowing is providing pertinent information. Let's discover how your claircognizance operates so that you can learn to rely on this part of yourself.

Explore Your Claircognizance

Claircognizance means clear knowing and provides instantaneous foresight that lets you know what is coming next. Interestingly, claircognizance is also the core instinct you rely on when you are born into the world. Having no knowledge of your environment, your knowingness instinctually tells you how to react. When you need to eat, your awareness prompts your tearful communications, garnering instant attention. When you need to sleep, your claircognizance will close your eyes, putting you at ease. Unfortunately, in our culture, clear knowing is also the skill trained out of you the quickest.

By the time you begin elementary school, you have been taught not to trust your inner guidance. Instead, you are encouraged to defer to outside sources or experts for direction. Unfortunately, this practice inadvertently steers you away from your intuition, throwing off your natural rhythms and timings. It's my opinion that our lack of self-trust is one of the major reasons so many of us are ill, depressed and lost in our lives.

Let's explore your claircognizance now. Remember that the purpose of this exercise is to understand how well this skill is working for you and to find out how much it needs development.

1. Start by allowing yourself to become comfortable and relaxed.
2. Think back to a time when you lost an item such as your keys, glasses, or jewelry and suddenly had a knowing of where they were and found them. Ask yourself, what part of me had the awareness – where did I sense it in my body? Go back into the feelings and sensations of that awareness and familiarize yourself with how your claircognizance shows up.

3. Next, remember an incident when someone presented a fact to you that you were sure was correct. Notice how your knowingness gave you the clue.

4. Now, recall a time when someone presented a fact to you as truth that you were sure was a lie. Pay attention to where the clear knowing comes from and to how your body and mind perceive it.

Go ahead and take a moment now to ask yourself a few questions and ponder or journal how well this intuitive faculty is functioning:

- How easy or difficult was it for me to recall a past claircognizant moment?

- Was I able to determine where that sense was taking place in my body?

- How did my clear knowing help me understand truth versus non-truth? Where did I sense it in my body?

- How can this skill help me in my everyday life?

Develop Your Claircognizance

A dear friend of mine once had a brilliant idea, which she proposed to her husband. She had heard of an up and coming franchise opportunity that she absolutely knew would be successful for them. The business consisted of a series of kiosks placed outside fast-food restaurants and convenience stores where people could purchase movie rentals. Unfortunately, my friend's husband didn't put much stock in her knowingness and passed on the idea. Now each time he drives by a RedBox, he cringes at the thought of the early retirement he passed up.

When you develop your sense of knowing, it not only allows you instant access to complete understanding, it also connects you to brilliant ideas. The steps below will aid you in expanding your higher awareness. However, if you find that this skill is overly active, don't feel that you have to practice it at this time.

1. One of the best ways to develop your claircognizance is to learn to be authentic. Sometimes in life, it's important to say what you really see, feel, hear, and know regardless of what others might think, even if two seconds later you want to change your mind. You can't sense truths until you hear your own. Speak what is on your mind. Be real.

2. Another way to hone your claircognizance is by allowing yourself to become quiet and empty before making important decisions. As you reach the point of stillness, you are opening your awareness beyond your mentally perceived reality, where claircognizance is strongest. Stay in that space of nothingness for a while, not searching for the answers to your life issue but absorbing solutions you didn't know were possible. When you emerge from your stillness, your claircognizance will be more active. As you go about your daily routines, your heightened sense will easily clue you in to the details of your life that need healing and the solutions that will set you free. Practice stillness and the ability to allow innovative ideas to soak in every day.

3. You can also develop your claircognizance by learning to trust, which is also why it can be more difficult to practice this step. Trust is a tricky issue for most people, as it places them in vulnerable positions. Yet by believing that your intuition will guide you to where you need to be, your claircognizance greatly amplifies, steering you gently on your path.

4. But also, don't be fearful of engaging with people, adventures and ideas. Assume a trusting nature in your daily interactions as well. Your knowingness will sense the truth of the events and people in your life so you can rest assured that you are safe.

Evolve Your Thinking

It's interesting how life cannot change until our thoughts shift into new beliefs. You might have thoughts about yourself that sound like these: "I don't trust myself," "I don't have the proper education to better myself," or

"I don't have the right to follow my personal truth." These thoughts create the beliefs that pattern your life experiences. It's important that you revise your negative ideas in order to create new circumstances. Replace your lower thoughts with any of the following higher ideas below, or generate the mantras you prefer.

"I trust that I have access to universal knowledge at all times."

"It's easy for me to hear truths and non-truths."

"It's best for me to adhere to my authenticity."

Claircognizance Accesses World-Changing Advancements

Did you know that many metaphysicians and scientists believe that ideas, inventions and life-altering technology exist as information hovering around us, awaiting our recognition and subsequent creation? However, scientists also say that this information isn't restricted to one person. They cite that throughout history many innovations often overlap.

Researchers state that at the time the Wright brothers mastered lift with the first airplane, inventors around the globe were discovering it as well. They also point to the time when Alexander Graham Bell invented the telephone. It would seem that several other inventors, such as Elisha Gray and Antonio Meucci, developed the same groundbreaking technology simultaneously, without knowledge of each other's work. You have to wonder, how could three men from varying backgrounds with no contact to one another conceptualize the same product?

Ideas are not exclusive to one person. It is widely recognized that individuals such as Leonardo da Vinci, Nicola Tesla, Albert Einstein and even Steve Jobs accredit many of their ideas to moments of instant knowingness and higher awareness. In that sense, these scientists were adept at using their claircognizant superpower to attune to universal innovations, bringing great advancements to the collective – and so can you.

Many advanced thinkers are already using their higher awareness to find innovative solutions to thinks like climate change. For instance, a British company has invented drones that can spray one billion tree seeds a year throughout ravaged forests as a way of restoring the environment. There are also ideas for a giant wind farm in the Atlantic Ocean that could generate enough power for all of humanity. Plans are even underway to begin cleaning plastic out of the oceans.

Your ability to gain access to transformative concepts is your final superpower, bringing sustainable solutions to life's most pressing issues. Are you paying attention? Would you be willing to capitalize on an idea that could improve your life and the lives of others? As you embrace your new superhuman abilities, you are ready to enter into your next intuitive phase.

You have now completed Part II. With your newfound understanding, you can start to alter your reality and make a bigger difference in the world. Make it a habit to inwardly see, hear, feel and know the world around you. Refer back to this chapter as often as you need as a way to ingrain these concepts in your everyday life

INTUITIVELY RESPONSIBLE

Assume Personal Power and Generate Collective Well-Being

"It is by logic that we prove, but by intuition that we discover."

– Henri Poincaré, French mathematician

OLIVIA WAS MY client and had a friend, Emily, who was in turmoil. Generously, Olivia gifted Emily a session with me in hopes that I could help. When I received the call from Olivia to purchase the session, she wanted me to know exactly what Emily's problem was – her father. Olivia went on to tell me how Emily's dad had instilled in Emily a sense of unworthiness and low self-esteem. As a result, Emily's relationships with men were abusive, unloving and non-supportive, and her financial prospects weren't any better. Consequently, she was increasingly becoming dependent on sleep medications and anti-depressants just to get through a day.

Yet as sweet as it was that Olivia wanted to make sure I understood Emily's plight, part of the ethics of being an intuitive practitioner requires that I not allow another person's perspective to influence my intuition. Honestly, I prefer not to know anything about a client's situation before I view it symbolically for myself. This ensures that my instincts are clear of bias prior to engaging in extensive dialogue. So while I listened to Olivia, I also reserved the right to gauge Emily's circumstances for myself.

When I finally met Emily, I found that, sadly, much of what Olivia had said was true. The lack of parental guidance in Emily's upbringing was causing profoundly negative implications in all aspects of her life. She had no love for herself and no love for life, and it showed in her unkempt appearance and her inability to look me in the eye. It was easy to see that Emily felt defeated. Nevertheless, I explained to Emily that her father wasn't truly the issue. The real problem Emily faced was that she had never received an education about the science of her intuition and was therefore living as a victim to her circumstances.

I mentioned earlier that scientists once believed that the earth, cosmos and all living things were birthed from a chemical reaction. This theory suggests that we are victims to what happens to us and are powerless to change our circumstances. Today, science tells a different story. We now understand that we are an energetic charge driven by our intentions. In that sense, victimhood no longer needs to dominate the landscapes of your life. Instead, you can gain control over your intentions and become the highly-empowered creator of your circumstances.

It helped Emily to understand that as a child, she might have been subject to the behaviors of the adults around her, but once matured, she could step into the role of architect of her life. Emily had never thought of herself as capable, let alone powerful enough to be in command of her own fate. She was eager to learn how her intuition could change her perception of herself and to discover what effect that could have on her ability to find purpose, love and happiness.

Emily immediately enrolled in my intuitive development classes. It took some time, but eventually her life transformed. Emily learned to admire her unique sensibilities, which enabled her to hold her head high and resulted in her establishing a sustainable career. She was even making new friends and was open to the idea that she deserved respect and love in partnership. It was thrilling to watch Emily finally come alive.

Do you know who you are outside of what others expect you to be? Interestingly, when I ask my clients this question, rarely do I get an accurate response. Generally, I hear accounts such as, "I'm a busy mom trying to keep everyone on track." "I'm a stressed-out corporate employee trying to meet a quota." "I'm an overworked, underpaid and burned-out social worker who just wants the world to heal." However, these types of descriptors only tell me what a person is obligated and expected to be, not who they are authentically.

Titles and expectations do not make you who you are. Your personal truths define you. What is the busy mom's truth? What does the stressed out employee really believe? And how effective does the burned-out professional truly feel? Most mothers don't want to be overly controlling; they just think society says that makes a good parent. Most people do not enjoy their jobs; they simply work out of necessity. And many individuals don't agree with the business politics of profit before people but feel that their hands are tied in making a difference.

There is a reason the lesser 99% of the world's population are not the elite 1%. The majority of people allow unrealistic ideals about what is important in life, such as fame, fortune, faith and many other things to distract them from fulfilling their higher ideals. Why? We are all Emily; victims to another person or organization's ideals, forgetting our personal power, although it doesn't have to be that way.

In this chapter, you will use your intuition to become responsible for your personal energetics and the circumstances they allow into your life. As you assume a higher command over your personal space, you naturally want to create equality, camaraderie and common ground, setting a higher and more harmonious standard for relating that changes your life and brings authenticity to the world.

Assume Your Innate Wisdom and Change Reality

"No man is free who is not a master of himself."

– Epictetus, Philosopher

ZOE HAD A TERRIBLE time making choices. Her constant worry that she might make a poor decision often caused her to take no action at all. Consequently, Zoe's severe indecisiveness was creating a burden on the people in her life, as they were reluctantly assuming responsibility for deciding her personal circumstances. Sadly, Zoe's boyfriend was no longer willing to be her keeper and had ended their three-year relationship. Needless to say, Zoe didn't know what to do.

Realizing the immense impact that Zoe's uncertainty was having in her life, I knew it was imperative that we connect her to her personal wisdom. One of the strategies I use to help students discover their higher awareness is to have them intuitively witness their energetic Command Central. If you have seen the Pixar film Inside Out you know what I'm talking about. The animated movie focuses on the main character's control center located in her mind, calling it headquarters, and which is responsible for creating all her experiences.

Like Joy, the Pixar character, you have a Command Central that is responsible for designing your circumstances as well. This space is reserved for only you and provides you access to universal knowledge so that you can determine your unique beliefs and life paths. The Sherlock Holmes character also uses something of this nature when he refers to his mind palace, an internal place where he goes in order to block out the rest of the world and deduce his ingenious solutions. Zoe needed to understand that she had this same type of mental refuge available to her that could help her make choices. However, not only was Zoe oblivious to the idea that she had a Command Central, when I looked to see what was happening in that space, I noticed it was jam packed with people and their expectations and was serving as anything but a sanctuary.

In order to help Zoe find her ability to choose wisely, I witnessed her Command Central room to see who was in charge. The space was overrun with wall-to-wall people. I recognized Zoe's family members, friends, teachers, and even the mail carrier inside her sacred space, all of them shouting commands for her to follow. It seemed to me that Zoe was helpless to change the situation, as if she felt she needed to defer to the better judgments of others.

I then listened for the loudest voice in the crowd, in hopes of finding the origin of Zoe's belief so we could shift it. I quickly isolated the frequency of a group of women in the middle of the room chanting, "Don't do the wrong thing, you'll never live it down." I felt that these females represented the women in Zoe's family and their collective fear of taking a wrong step.

Interestingly, when I shared my insights about her Command Central, Zoe explained that all her life she had received warnings from her grandmother, aunts and mother about the implications of making a bad choice. Apparently, teen pregnancy, alcoholism and even being large-boned ran in the family, creating perceived hardship and, therefore, lower circumstances for the women. Consequently, Zoe grew up deluged with worries, anxieties and fears about how she wasn't smart or pretty enough to know what was best for herself. Unfortunately, while the intentions of the women in Zoe's family were well-meaning and meant to keep her on a straight and narrow path, the impact of her generational programming was causing her to doubt her ability to be wise, immobilizing her from choosing her life's experiences.

When lower thinking is at play, right or wrong becomes the perception. However, intuition tells us that all experiences, good and bad, serve a purposeful function in our growth. I was a teen mother. While some people might perceive my pregnancy as being the result of bad choices, it was my saving grace and therefore exactly what I needed.

Intuition does not subscribe to the idea that one experience is greater than another. It knows that all expressions are necessary to bring us to our truths and growth. Zoe needed permission to make her own choices based on her personal beliefs and desires if she was going to know herself well enough to maintain a healthy relationship. This would require that she reclaim her Command Central room.

Guiding Zoe inwardly, I first instructed her to remove all the people from her room, as this would establish her authority as the creator of her reality. After having Zoe perform her intuitive maintenance, she was then to check in with her room several times throughout the day to ensure that no one had slipped in, having undue influence over her. With her head clear, Zoe could now practice making her own decisions by not turning to others for advice.

I suggested that Zoe be still and focus her attention into her Command Central prior to forming her choices. There she could contemplate her options without interference, revisiting the space as often as needed until she felt certain about a path. Once she made a decision, she was to waste no time enacting her desires. Ultimately, this practice would orient Zoe to her personal truth and her ability to act in her own best interest. Whether the decision turned out to be positive or negative was somewhat irrelevant, as each experience was leading her toward her growth. However, I also assured

Zoe that she was more than smart enough not to be reckless in her life and that if something went awry she could learn from it and shift course.

When you are not operating your Command Central, you are not in control of your reality, and other people can have unwarranted sway over you. Other people's authority may cause you anxiety, depression and uncertainty about your life's path and may even prevent you from acting on your dreams. Explore your Command Central now to determine if you are in charge of your reality or what you might need to do to assume your right to personal wisdom.

Discover Your Personal Authority

Your Command Central is your point of authority, your personal headquarters overseeing your driving forces and the reality they create. This room also gives you access to universal knowledge. Interestingly, many ancient cultures understood this concept of retreating into one's Command Central in order to discover new ideas and solutions. The Egyptians and Sumerians specifically created elaborate monuments and depictions of this inward space, believing it to be associated with the thalamus and pineal glands, which are located in the center of the brain. They even depicted these glands in art and sculpture, as if it were a sacred tool.

Interestingly, French philosopher René Descartes regarded the pineal gland as the place where the soul resides in the body. He also believed that it was in this gland that thoughts formed and life initiated. Descartes states, "The pineal gland is the focal point of our spiritual guiding system which makes us go beyond the five senses of rationality and become multisensory, tuned into and aware of higher dimensions of consciousness within a holographic cosmos."[xii]

If ancient cultures and philosophers idolized a gland we know little about today, it must have been important in ways we have forgotten and are only beginning to remember. Fortunately, you don't have to know anything about your pineal gland in order for it to work on your behalf as well as on behalf of humankind. Let's design your Command Central room now and activate your power now.

1. Allow yourself to relax, closing your eyes and placing your attention in the center of your mind, or within your pineal gland. Notice that this room is larger on the inside, offering you access to the infinite universe.

2. Using four cornerstone senses of clairvoyance, clairaudience, clairsentience, and claircognizance, begin to build and design your room in any way that feels right to you. Keep in mind that your room can be anywhere you desire and isn't bound by rules. You can also change your space any time you choose. My space is set in a faraway valley surrounded by mountains, has only two walls and is open to nature.

3. Once you have the location and foundation for your room, start to decorate the space with items that make you happy, like pictures, bright colors, knickknacks, furnishings, etc. My room has all the comforts of home.

4. Next, take a moment and design an intuitive viewing area within your space. This area is a specific part of your room where you will go to send and receive intuitive information as its function is to provide you with your own personal connection to universal wisdom. My intuitive viewing arena is in a movie theater with a large screen, surround sound and, of course, popcorn. When I want to sense an aspect of my life or when working with clients, I go to my movie theater and turn on my intuitive viewing screen so that I am able to discern my personal perspective and truth about a situation. Design a space for yourself like this now.

5. When complete take some time to see, hear, feel or know who is in your room, whether it's family, friends, colleagues, clergy, crossed-over loved ones or your favorite pet. As you witness who and what is in your room, ask yourself what type of influence each might be having in your life.

6. When you have a good understanding of who is in your space, regardless of whether they are well meaning or not, ask them to leave. The point is that this space exists so you can find sovereignty and personal truth, which are the keys to fulfillment. By reserving a space in your Command Central strictly for yourself, you are symbolically telling the universe that you are an individual being, assuming your right to higher knowledge. Go ahead now and escort out anyone in your room. If you find they are unwilling to leave, be assertive. Use something like a trap door to help them leave, not giving them an option. From now on, reserve this area exclusively for yourself, as this is how to be responsible and live the life of your choosing.

After you have claimed your authority and designed your Command Central room, reflect or journal on your experience as a means of gaining more understanding of this tool. Ask yourself:

- Where was my Command Central located?
- What was the design of the space?
- Where did I place my intuitive view area? What does it resemble?
- Who were the people in my Command Central room? What type of influence are they having in my life?
- How might my life be different without those influences?
- How does it feel to have a sacred space just for myself?
- How will this room help me in my everyday life?

Maintain Your Personal Authority

When I first learned the intuitive practice of being my own authority, I felt an enormous sense of freedom. Never before had I had permission for my personal truth. Honestly, I was used to the opposite. All my life, I had been told that my opinions didn't matter and that I should be quiet and do as I was told. The realization that my beliefs were just as valid as anyone else's empowered me in ways I didn't even know I needed.

Commanding my authority and owning my truth suddenly put me on equal footing with the rest of the world. No longer did I need to comply, being neither seen nor heard. Instead, I had a new resolve. I could pick up my head and let the world know who I was and what I believed. Suddenly, people perceived me differently and started allowing me my voice. Consequently, my business increased exponentially, and my personal relationships deepened immensely. However, just because I built my Command Central and cleared out the influence of other people once didn't mean I was finished with this intuitive tool. If I were to sustain my new sense of self, I would have to perform regular maintenance in this space.

Being your own authority allows you to be the leader of your life, accessing universal wisdom for yourself and others. You will want to perform routine checkups on your Command Central as a means for staying on track with your higher goals and ideals. Follow the intuitive practices below to learn how best to maintain your command:

1. The key to maintaining your Command Central room is to remain aware of what is taking place within that space. You can do this simply by placing your awareness on your room and checking in with it to make sure there is no one but you in there. If you see someone or something, make them leave. Later you can determine what type of influence they were having over your life and decide how to negate or instill that quality for yourself.

2. Another tool you might find exceptionally helpful is setting your crown, or point of energetic command, to the color of your personal authority. You can think of your crown as an energy halo. When I check in with my room to ensure my sovereignty, I set my crown to a dark orange color that deepens into a dark brownish-red, as that is the color I've found that represents my personal authority. What is your color for personal authority? Close your eyes and use all your inner senses of sight, sound, feeling, and knowing to

discover your power color. When you find your color, set your crown to reflect your self-command.

Evolve Your Thinking

As usual, it is always a good idea to recognize the thoughts you have about this intuitive concept. Take a moment to uncover the thoughts within you that have a negative spin, such as "I'm not smart enough to be an authority," "I don't have the right to assert myself," or "My way is the only way." Shift the thoughts to something positive and inclusive. You can use one of my suggestions, or compose phrases that suit you best.

"I know what is in my best interest."

"Everything I do is right even when it's not."

"We are all authorities and have access to the same universal knowledge."

Assert Your Personal Authority and Become Equals with the World

When you read the story of Zoe and her inability to make a choice, you gained a deeper understanding of how one person's disempowerment creates a hardship for everyone. Thankfully, Zoe changed the world the day she assumed her personal responsibility and started making her own life choices. By not relying on others to choose her experiences, she not only engaged her individual evolution, she lessened the burden she was placing on others, freeing them to pursue their greater growth as well.

One of the largest trends shifting the world today is our willingness to embrace equality in all people. Of course, you cannot have equality without personal responsibility first. Thankfully, intuition affords you the benefit of becoming the authority of your life, allowing you to see yourself as an equal to others, as well as seeing others as your equivalent. Now that you have a stronger understanding of how to assume personal responsibility, you can establish a higher standard of operating for yourself, sending a ripple of transformative energy to everyone around you that they can do the same for themselves as well.

Command Your Circumstances in Ways that Benefit All

"The difference between one man and another is not mere ability… it is energy."

– Thomas Arnold, Historian

MARIE WAS AT A networking event when she met Hanna. Hanna was sweet, upbeat, and outgoing and approached Marie in hopes that Marie would consider using her accounting services. The only problem was that Hanna was strangely unconscious of the concept of personal space. She stood nearly nose-to-nose with Marie, making her exceptionally uncomfortable. Thankfully, Marie had been studying intuitive development and had recently learned how to take charge of her energy field.

As Marie stood breathless and face-to-face with Hanna, intuitively she put a symbolic bubble around her energetic field. Once she placed the barrier around herself, she began to expand it to the edges of the room in order to feel less confined. Interestingly, Hanna unconsciously took a couple steps backward, as if subconsciously in tune with the influence gently nudging her away.

Marie was relieved and impressed. She later told me that although she had been enjoying her intuitive education, she hadn't really thought it could have much impact in her life until she witnessed how powerful her intentions could be in creating her ideal circumstances.

I've certainly had moments when people have infringed on my personal space, and I'm sure you have as well. How do you handle this type of situation? What if there was a way to give yourself what you need without taking anything away from others or making them wrong? Spirit tells us that we are all connected and, in that sense, we are ONE . . . my energy mingles with yours and yours with mine. But physically we are also individual and must recognize every person's right to their unique expression. Claiming your personal energy field and agreeing to assume command of it allows you to establish further both personal and collective balance. Explore your energetic field now, and take the next step toward your empowerment.

Claim Your Energetic Field

Your energetic field does more than create an energetic barrier around you. Your field serves as the container that houses and regulates your multi-dimensionality. You may not know it but you have many natures within you ranging from light to dark, masculine to feminine, and even sinner to saint. The energetic expressions you draw upon to create your life exist within your container of being. Taking command of your space is one of the keys to managing your equilibrium and sense of self. Follow the intuitive practices below to take responsibility for your energy so that you can have greater control over your personal experiences while also having a positive effect on the world.

1. Begin by closing your eyes and becoming still.
2. Using your cornerstone senses to envision, hear, feel and command that a symbolic bubble surround you, generally arm's length from your body.
3. Once you have your sphere defined, notice how you feel inside it, taking note of what it is like to have personal space and sovereignty.

4. Next, start to expand your field as large as you can. See if you can inflate it to the size of your state. Know that in an infinite universe, you can have as much space and energy as you need without taking it away from anyone else. In fact, every person can have as much energy as he or she requires.

5. When you have expanded your bubble, notice how you feel within the space. Gauge if you think you can manage that amount of energy or if it feels overwhelming or unruly.

6. Now contract your field, bringing it within inches of your body. Notice how you feel within that space, and notice whether or not you can organize and maintain a small amount of energy.

7. When you have completed both comparisons, allow your field to expand to whatever size feels easy to manage.

Take a moment to reflect on this simple exercise, as this will aid you in gaining greater awareness of how this intuitive tool works for you. Ask yourself the questions below for increased clarity:

- How easy or difficult was it to create my bubble? Why?
- How did I feel inside my energetic field?
- When I expanded my space, how did I feel? Could I easily manage that amount of energy?
- When I contracted my field, how did I feel? How comfortable was a smaller amount of energy?
- What was my energy bubble's natural size? Did that space feel manageable to me?
- How will taking charge of my energetic field help me in my everyday circumstances?

Maintain Your Energetic Field

I started noticing the need to manage my energetic field after volunteering at a music festival. I had been learning my intuitive skills but didn't necessarily use them in my everyday life yet. However, after one day of what was going to be a three-day event, I realized that I was going to have to put a bubble around me if I was going to make it through the weekend.

The problem was that I never had a moment's rest. Attendance at the festival was record high. I was busy from sun-up to sun-down. Consequently, I overloaded my personal space with everyone else's energy at the fair, exhausting myself. On day two, I made a point to isolate my energy field from the public, consciously serving people while also taking care of myself. Thankfully, it worked. Not only was I able to get through the day easily and with less fatigue, but I was able to maintain enthusiasm and a happiness to accommodate everyone's requests.

As you can see, establishing your personal space allows you to remain sovereign while still being in collaboration with others. This ability to be separate but work together is a major key to creating harmonious experiences in the world. Follow the two simple understandings below to maintain your energetic field anytime, anywhere:

1. As you go about your everyday life, don't forget to play with your field. Consciously expand and contract your space based on the circumstances you find yourself in. For example, if you are walking on a crowded street, expand your bubble so that you feel comfortable. If you are with your partner, bring your energy space in so that you feel cozy. The point is to use this intuitive skill as a means of managing your personal energy levels better.

2. As with all the tools in this book, you must apply these concepts in your everyday life if you desire to change your reality. In order to ingrain the idea of managing your personal space, it's best to consistently and consciously pay attention to your field and to how you are holding it. The best way I've found to do this is to change my bubble each time I change physical locations. For instance, I put a bubble around me before I begin working with clients. When I leave my office, I put a new energetic field around my car and me. I even put a new bubble around myself when I go into the grocery

store. This way I am being conscious of my expressions and surroundings, and I'm taking charge of creating higher circumstances.

Evolve Your Thinking

While claiming your energetic field is a necessary step, you will also need to address the thoughts you have regarding this concept of owning your space in order to ingrain a new pattern for yourself. Listen for the thoughts within you that sound like this: "I don't have a right to my sovereignty," "I don't have a right to what is best for me," or "It is fine if other people take up my space." The key now is to shift those thoughts toward something more positive and supportive. You can use the following mantras to replace your lower thoughts, or you can compose a phrase that best supports your unique circumstances.

"Owning my space makes me happier."

"My bubble keeps me safe."

"I can have as much space as I need."

Use Higher Awareness to Generate Safe Arenas for Others

I never realized the power energetic bubbles had in creating positive change in the world until the day I received notice that my middle son, the U.S. Marine, had stepped on an improvised explosive device (IED) in Afghanistan. My son's foot needed to be amputated that day, and he now wears a prosthetic. However, his injuries were far less severe than they should have been with little explanation as to why, except for the fact that I had put a bubble around him to keep him safe.

From the time my son was born, he was going to be a Marine. Despite my insistence that he choose another path, at age eighteen he left home to go to war. As a concerned mother, I naturally feared for his life. As a knowledgeable intuitive, I began asking the angels, saints and spirits of every person in my family to protect him.

Then one day while I was driving to my office, I had an unexpected vision of my Marine being blown up. In a panic, I did the only thing I could do from thousands of miles away. I put my baby in an energetic bubble, surrounding him with love, protection and prayers, hoping I was just being paranoid. Two weeks later, I received the dreadful call informing me that my son had been injured. Thankfully, I also learned that his injuries were somewhat minimized and could have been much worse. It would seem that only 40% of the explosive my son stepped on ignited, sparing him from shrapnel wounds and head, neck and back injuries common among wounded warriors. Consequently, my son's only physical injury was his shattered ankle, which couldn't be saved.

Six weeks and multiple surgeries later, I transferred my son from Walter Reed Memorial Hospital in Washington, D.C. to Balboa Naval Hospital in San Diego, California so that he could be closer to home. Interestingly, the first physician at Balboa to examine my son was surprised that he had only lost his foot given the scope of injuries he was used to seeing. The doctor was so impressed that he looked at my son and matter-of-factly said, "Have you ever heard of being shielded? I think that's what happened to you." I was shocked to have a medical professional acknowledge the etheric realities.

I believe my energetic efforts to shield my son helped to minimize the event. However, I also know I could not have prevented the incident, as the experience was necessary for my son's personal evolution. I honestly feel that if it had been my son's time to depart, he would have died no matter how hard I prayed or protected him. I can't tell you how grateful I am every day that my noble son's path was to survive so that he could change his stance on war.

One of the keys to mending the world is to allow your intuition to lend consciousness and healing to others where needed in order to make a greater difference in the world. I now put all the people I love in protective fields just to cover all the bases. I even put fields around strangers I pass on the street if I think they are experiencing difficulties or are in danger. If you feel helpless to stop world hunger, put a bubble of abundance and peace around the earth. If you feel helpless to stop government corruption and manipulation, put a bubble of transparency around your federal and state offices and even your elected officials. As you energetically offer positive energy to the world's plights, you are providing clarity and consciousness to all, which in turn enables people to rise above their limiting expressions. In that sense, know that you are absolutely working with the trends that are creating a better world.

Determine Your Parameters and Build Healthy Relationships

"Your personal boundaries protect the inner core of your identity and your right to choices."

– Gerard Manley Hopkins, English poet

LIBBY WAS A HAIR stylist with a big heart who couldn't say no to the demands of her clients, family and friends. Consequently, Libby was exhausted, stressed and was even overweight to the point of experiencing ill health. She wanted to know what she could do to improve her personal circumstances. When I intuitively witnessed Libby's situation, I immediately recognized that Libby's problem wasn't her life's many expectations. The issue was that Libby was an empath who suffered from the ailment often referred to by metaphysicians as No Boundary Syndrome. Thankfully, the cure to this phenomenon is simple, fun and exceptionally powerful in establishing personal parameters that create healthy relationships.

Everyone is empathic to some degree. However, empaths are highly sensitive individuals whose clairsentient skill is overly active. As a result, these individuals unknowingly feel and respond to the emotions and energies of those around them, even taking responsibility for other people's issues as if they were their own. If you are shaking your head in agreement because you relate to the above statement, you are empathic. It's likely that, like Libby, you suffer from No Boundary Syndrome as well and need to practice protecting your energetic field with the techniques presented in this chapter. If this doesn't sound like you, then you are more like me.

If you recall, feeling was not my strongest intuitive skill. I don't consider myself naturally clairsentient. However, even if you are not in the habit of assuming the emotions of others, establishing boundaries is essential to creating your ideal health, fulfillment and purpose, as they allow you to define symbolically for the universe how you wish to experience the circumstances of your life.

Libby would need to understand that in order for her fatigue, ill health and finances to improve, she was going to have to learn to establish healthy boundaries. These energetic restrictions would ensure that each person in her life was being responsible for their own growth and was not taking more from Libby than she had to give.

In my session with Libby, I taught her how to use her intuition to establish healthy personal parameters. By putting specific symbols around her energetic field, she would be defining the types of experiences she wished to have with her clients, family and friends. I suggested that Libby surround her energy in a protective shield with signs reading, "Do not trespass," and "Keep out." With an energetic boundary such as this in place, Libby would be emitting a sort of barrier that would naturally cause the energies of those around her to minimize their demands. More importantly, these boundaries would also ensure that she would be less likely to rescue others needlessly.

Another idea I offered Libby was to surround her energy field with a symbolic boundary of roses. Roses typically symbolize universal beauty, love and honor for self and others. However, roses also have thorns, which is great because they cause people to subconsciously think twice before haphazardly interfering with your energies. However, Libby wasn't limited to using the boundaries I suggested. She was free to find the parameters that suited her personally. Libby liked the idea that she could use any symbolic imagery that felt right to her to define her space. She was excited to use this tool in her everyday life.

As Libby practiced using boundaries, she quickly noticed that she not only had more time and energy, but also her business began to increase and her health started to improve. However, the greatest result Libby noticed was how her energy protections were allowing her clients and family members to become less dependent on her and, more importantly, motivated to do for themselves.

Do you use boundaries in your life? What might happen if you did? The greatest thing I've noticed about setting energetic parameters is that it not only makes you more responsible for your energy but also causes the people you interact with to be responsible for their essence as well. Follow the exploration below, and learn how to define your ideal reality.

Explore Your Boundaries

In the last chapter, you learned how to define your energetic field. Now, let's learn to use energetic boundaries to protect your space and regulate the types of experiences you encounter. It's important to note that you can use anything as a boundary, like flowers, trees, crystals, mirrors, or feathers. You can also use walls, moats, and other distance-creating boundaries that isolate you, but realize the ramifications of such things: trees are inclusive, but walls are isolating. You will want to consciously determine the parameter appropriate to the situation.

When I first learned to set boundaries, roses were what I used. However, over the years, I've also adopted many other types of symbols for boundaries. When I am around difficult people, I put mirrors around my energy field that reflect outward toward others so that they energetically see themselves during our interactions and are not focusing their energy on me. I find that this aids people in being less defensive and angry so that we can have mutually respectful conversations. I also immerse myself within a large diamond when I am hosting an intuitive session with clients. Diamonds are exceptionally hard and don't allow energy to penetrate. At the same time, they are clear, so I can still see my client's situations plainly without taking on their issues as my own.

I recommend changing your boundaries for each of your circumstances. When I'm with friends, I put a barrier of roses around myself so that I can connect but still maintain my sense of self. When I am with strangers, I hold a boundary of redwood trees around me. This not only aids me in feeling grounded and secure with myself but also sets a standard of strength, endurance and self-reliance so that others perceive my capabilities and don't feel the need to rescue or manage me. When I'm with my partner, I have a boundary of silk feathers designed to connect deeply – like birds of a feather. Go ahead and explore your boundaries now with the intuitive practices outlined below:

1. Start by closing your eyes and putting a bubble around your energetic field.

2. Once you have your field defined, put a boundary of roses around your field. Be sure and use all your intuitive senses to see, hear, feel and know your boundaries. Pay attention to how you feel when you are surrounded by roses and how they allow you to interact with others.

3. When you have gotten a good understanding of how roses feel as boundaries, change them to mirrors reflecting away from you. Notice how mirrors affect your space differently from roses and how that might change your interactions with others.

4. Next, put a brick wall around your energetic space and notice what that does to you and your ability to interact with others.

5. When you've given yourself time to feel what it is like to have walls up, put whatever parameters around you that feel best, whether you have explored it earlier or have come up with something for yourself.

6. Remember, you can change your boundaries and likely should whenever you change your settings.

Now that you have established your boundaries, take a moment to reflect on your experiences. Ask yourself how this skill is working for you.

- How easy or difficult was it to set my boundaries?
- What boundaries worked best for me? Why?
- How will boundaries help me in my everyday circumstances?

Maintain Your Boundaries

Keep in mind that boundaries are pointless if you don't apply them to your everyday circumstances. This is why the best thing you can do to support your energetic parameters is tell the people in your life that you have boundaries.

I remember once drawing a line with my boys. I had spent the entire weekend cleaning the house, top to bottom, including their rooms and bathroom. By Sunday evening, I was finally finishing all my chores. While putting away the last of the laundry, I went into the boys' bathroom and, shockingly, it was disgusting. It looked as if I hadn't been in there for months. Not only had they used the toilet and missed, but they had also left mud on the floors and walls, and I think there were even crayfish in the tub. That was it for me. I grabbed my cleaning supplies, marched over to my children and told them I would never clean up after them again. I explained that they were old enough to be responsible for their surroundings, and then I handed them the tools to clean up after themselves.

In that moment, I claimed what I needed and set a boundary that was never crossed. Had I said nothing, I would probably be cleaning their adult homes today. Instead, they learned the value of cleanliness, and I got some much-needed time for fun. Seemed like a win-win to me. Below is a set of intuitive practices you can use to enact and expand your boundaries:

1. To begin, get used to using boundaries every day. While you are driving, spending time at work or lounging at home, be aware of how you are holding your space and of how that affects your reality.

2. Also, change your boundaries each time you move into a new setting. Then give attention to your parameters often to ensure that they are operating effectively for you.

3. Yet the most effective way to maintain your boundaries is to express to the people in your life what protections you are adopting for yourself. This isn't necessarily easy, but when you express from your heart what you've decided you need to feel good in your life, you really can't be denied.

4. But also don't be afraid to change a boundary that isn't really serving you. If you are actively seeking a romantic partner yet invoke a boundary of extreme independence, competence and perfection, you might find it hard to meet an ideal mate. Perhaps surrounding your energy in a light of self-esteem, acceptance and trust would allow you to attract the right person. In other words, don't be afraid to be honest with yourself. If your boundaries are too harsh or too soft, they can't serve you well. Find the boundaries that are just right for the life you want to lead.

Evolve Your Thinking

Now that you know how to enact boundaries, consider the thoughts you have regarding your personal parameters. Sort through your mind's data bank and find the negative thoughts that say, "It will upset other people if I use my boundaries," "Boundaries are too difficult to maintain," or "I don't like people and wish I could build a wall to keep them out." Once you've isolated your limiting thoughts, shift them to something supportive. You can insert one of the following higher ideas or develop your own.

"Boundaries make everyone responsible for their own life."

"I have more energy and feel better when I use boundaries."

"People respect me more when I have boundaries."

Use Protective Parameters Around Others to Aid in Their Betterment

Many years ago, I realized that even though I surrounded myself in boundaries, I would occasionally experience the very circumstances I was trying to avoid. For instance, I once purposely protected my space in such a way as to avoid overly intrusive women. However, the minute I invoked my boundaries, suddenly every woman I met was in need of more than I could give. I started to question why my boundaries were not holding. What I learned was a life lesson I never expected.

I used to have a girl friend who was very expectant of me. I often felt our friendship was predicated on the idea that I would adhere to all her needs and desires whenever her fancy struck. Unfortunately, being the mother of three boys, you can imagine I didn't have time for such a demanding friendship. Not wanting to hurt my friend's feelings, I said nothing but started using stronger boundaries with her.

I would surround myself in mirrors that faced outward when I was with my friend, hoping she would see her unreasonable behaviors for herself. It never worked. I also began using walls for boundaries; but again, no luck. I then decided to speak my boundaries, making it clear to her that I could not respond to all her needs, to which she yelled, "As my friend, you owe me time!"

As I paused in bewilderment at what would be my friend's final demand of me, I learned an invaluable lesson. Intuitively, as I pondered why my boundaries were not being effective with her, I heard my higher awareness say, "because this tension will make you put yourself first for a change."

I had always been in the habit of putting the needs of others ahead of my own. However, I was being given the opportunity to shift that aspect of myself and no boundary I set was going to get in the way of my progress. It would seem that the reason overbearing women were a constant theme in my life was because they were helping me stand up for myself, which is exactly what I did in that moment with my friend when I ended our relationship. Now the women I encounter are positive, supportive and more importantly, not looking to monopolize my time.

It would seem that boundaries do not always stop you from experiencing negative circumstances. Sometimes you need disruptive events to generate your higher awareness and growth. With this understanding, I started to use my boundaries differently. At times when I would encounter less than ideal situations, instead of trying to eliminate the negativity, I started surrounding my energetic field with a childlike light of awe and wonder. Shifting my stance allowed me to glean the purpose of my interactions in those moments, such as learning to maintain my personal power in the face of imposing figures, so that I could grow into a greater sense of self.

One of the best ways to assist in the transformation of the world is to change the attitude you have about it. Just as hate breeds hate and war breeds war, your frustration causes others to become defensive, creating discord rather than peace, often extending the issue much longer than necessary. However, using boundaries to regulate how you will allow an experience to affect you is one of easiest ways to honor other people while still adhering to your own needs, bringing peace to the world.

Embody Reality and Bring Your Higher Purpose to the World

"The secret of health for both mind and body is not to mourn for the past, worry about the future, or anticipate troubles, but to live in the present moment wisely and earnestly."

– Buddha

ETTA DESPERATELY needed a career. Her twelve-year marriage had ended. Although the court system awarded her five years of maintenance, she only had two years remaining. More frustrating was the fact that despite having two masters' degrees, although neither of which she used professionally, she had been unsuccessful in finding work and establishing her financial future.

When I first looked at Etta's energy, I immediately noticed that her spirit did not inhabit her body, rendering her unable to access her will to be motivated. This type of disassociation happens to many people. They have a resistance to a life challenge or to the effort they will need to apply in order to accomplish a goal, causing their spirit to disconnect from their tangible reality.

Energetically, your higher purpose is to bring your spirit into physical form. Your spirit carries within it all your potentials, opportunities and inspirations. Your body carries within it density, time, and the ability to manifest tangle elements in a physical plane. When both spirit and body combine their gifts, your life and the span of your influence becomes limitless. However, when your body is devoid of your spirit, you will experience difficulties and will be unable to create sustainable solutions.

If you want to be effective in creating your reality, you must be present, which means that your spirit and body are united and working in tandem. After ensuring that Etta understood this larger concept, I offered her some intuitive tools to use that would teach her how to be present and invigorated so that she could manifest a financial future.

Etta wisely applied these tools to her life. Every morning for six weeks, she practiced grounding, releasing and anchoring her spirit into her body at the start of her day. When she finished her energy renewal routine, Etta purposefully left the dishes in the sink and the laundry unfolded and, instead, devoted two to three hours solely on being present to the ideas and needs of career and finance. Etta redesigned her resume, sent out cover letters, and made job inquiries in an effort to build energy toward her desires. Once Etta finished with the material aspects of her day, she was free to let her spirit roam.

I'm happy to say that it wasn't long before Etta's ability to be present in her life resulted in a job. She found a position with a small research firm where she could ease into the industry and become comfortable earning a living. However, Etta didn't stop her morning energy ritual once she found a job. She continued to use her grounding and anchoring intuitive tools every morning as a form of personal maintenance as the practice filled her with a general sense of motivation and enthusiasm.

Do you have a hard time creating your ideal circumstances? Do you feel grounded in your life? What might happen if you anchor into reality? Manifestation only occurs in present time. In this section, you will learn the powerful tools of grounding, releasing and renewing so that you can be present to manifest your higher needs.

Recycle Your Energy

Grounding was not my first instinct. I have had to learn to ground and renew my energy several times a day as a way of staying in my body so that I can manifest my life. Thankfully, this practice is easy, painless and exceptionally rejuvenating. While there are many aspects to this powerful technique, once you are familiar with them, you can quickly ground and become present to manifest in a blink of an eye. Follow the steps below to explore how to ground and renew your energy.

<u>What you need to know prior to exploring this intuitive technique:</u>

1. Grounding and renewing is a three-step process. First, you must energetically establish a grounding cord, then you must use that cord to release all the energy from your field, followed by renewing yourself with life-giving energy.

2. Your energetic grounding cord connects at your hips, and anchors to the core of the earth, serving two purposes. First, your cord allows your spirit to connect to your body and the earth keeping you in present time. This enables you to manifest your desires into the physical world. Second, your grounding cord allows you to release energy from your field, freeing yourself of tired, worn-out energy so you can stay in flow.

3. You can establish your cord using any symbol you like. For instance, you can use a tree trunk, a flower stem, a titanium conduit, crystals or even a column of light. Often it's best to use a natural and organic cord so that you feel like a part of the earth.

4. However, feel free to play with this tool to find what makes you feel present and able to create your ideal circumstances.

5. Once you have grounded, you will use your grounding cord to release the energy from your field. When your space is empty, you can bring your energy back, revitalizing yourself. Let's try this exercise now.

How to recycle your energy: Creating a grounding cord

1. Start by closing your eyes and envisioning your grounding cord, such as a tree, crystal, light or water. Connect this cord to your hips and to the core of the earth. This action symbolically tells the universe that you wish to be in the present moment on earth, manifesting in a physical reality.

2. Using all your intuitive senses, observe your grounding cord taking note of how it feels, what it looks like, how it connects and flows.

3. Next, cut off your cord letting it fall down and release from your space. Take a moment to notice what it feels like to be ungrounded, not tethered to earth and physicality.

4. Now give yourself another grounding cord. You can use the same thing or something different, but initiate a new connection from your hips to the earth's core. Again, take note of how you feel when grounded in present time, and notice what type of grounding feels best to you.

How to recycle your energy: Releasing your energy

1. Start by closing your eyes, claiming your personal energy field and putting boundaries around your space.

2. Next, recognize that you have a grounding cord and that it's connected to your hips and to the center of the earth. Open your cord so that it is hollow on the inside.

3. With a hollow connection, command that all the energy in your field be released down your grounding cord. Be sure and release fully, letting everything go. This means that people, children, ideas, projects, stress, ill health, etc. must be removed from your field. The point is to reach a state of nothingness. When your field is empty and nothing is calling your attention, you will feel a sense of perfection, as if all is right. It's important that you stay in this place for a moment, allowing yourself to fully decompress from your life's

demands. The minute you think about your life circumstances, the energies will return. For now, enjoy your sovereignty.

4. Once you have released all your energy, you are ready to renew and reinvent yourself. Begin by envisioning a golden sun above your head. The sun serves as a symbolic representation of new life and rebirth. With the sun above you, ask to have all the energy that you released into the earth come back into your sun. You can watch as the stream of energy comes out of the earth and into the sun. The sun will churn and renew your energy, giving life to it again. As you witness your energy filtering into your personal star, watch it grow and expand with your essence. If there is any aspect of yourself or your life that you would like to reinvent, this is the time to incorporate new energy into your system. For instance, if I feel I need to be less serious, I will ask to have the energy of playfulness come into my sun. This way when I fill myself in, I'm also getting an extra dose of whimsy.

5. Once your sun is full, you can simply pop it like a balloon and allow all the energy to come into your head, neck and shoulders. Then allow the radiant energy to continue to fill up your chest, arms, hips, and legs and flow all the way to the tips of your toes. The point is to completely fill in your energetic field with life-giving force. At this time, you should feel refreshed and ready to handle any challenge the day brings.

6. Practice this idea of grounding, releasing and renewing as often as you can throughout the day as a means of staying present, alert and motivated.

To further ingrain these techniques, contemplate and/or journal your reactions to the following questions:

- What did I use for a grounding cord? Why?
- What did it feel like to be ungrounded?
- What did it feel like to be grounded?

- How easy or difficult was it to release all my energy down my grounding cord? Why?
- How did it feel to be completely released and in a state of perfection? How can being emptied out and in a state of nothingness help me?
- How easy or difficult was it to establish a sun? Was I able to fill in myself easily?
- How does grounding help me in my everyday circumstances?
- How does releasing help me in my daily routines?
- How does filling myself in and renewing my energy help me in my life?

Maintain Your Renewable System

Just as boundaries can be tricky to maintain, grounding can be a challenge for many reasons. I've often noticed that people who are in a lot of pain or are preparing to die will disconnect their grounding so that their spirit doesn't have to endure what the body is going through. Addicts, when in the midst of their high, will also be out of their bodies, living in their fantasy. Your spirit will even detach from its physical form when you are at work and your mind wanders, wishing you were elsewhere. Unfortunately, when your spirit does not inhabit your body, it's very difficult to bring your desires to fruition.

It would be wise to develop and sustain your ability to ground and renew your energy. It not only helps you stay in present time so that you can manifest your ideal reality, but it also revitalizes all aspects of your daily routines. Below is a set of intuitive practices you can use to expand and develop your ability to ground and renew.

1. Practice grounding, releasing and renewing your energy often throughout the day. If you are stopped at a red light, on hold with support, or getting ready to make dinner, take a moment to recycle your energies. You don't have to take a lot of time with this tool;

you can simply intend to be grounded, released and renewed. It will happen that quickly – energy follows intention.

2. You can also practice grounding other aspects of your life. I often give my car a grounding cord as a way of establishing greater control over myself on the road. I will even ground my office, house or children as a way of assisting positive flow. Play with this concept for yourself. You certainly cannot harm anyone or anything by using this tool.

Evolve Your Thinking

The last step to mastering the concept of grounding and renewing is being aware of the thoughts you have about these concepts. Find the thoughts within you that say, "I don't like to be grounded and just want to be free," "I feel bad releasing my family and children," or "I'm too tired to go out." Shift your lower ideals. Consider inserting the following higher thoughts in place of your lower ones. Of course, you can develop you own sayings as well.

"Grounding feels good and allows me to accomplish my higher goals."

"Releasing the people I love allows them to know themselves as well."

"I'm brave and enter the world, because that is where I will find my life's answers."

Allow Your Presence to Contribute to the Collective's Higher Goals

Using the intuitive techniques of grounding and renewing your energy can clear your mind, anchor your spirit, and emotionally engage you. However, of all the benefits grounding offers, applying purposeful effort toward the world's higher goals is one of the greatest. While many spiritual practices emphasize being as the way to personal enlightenment, doing is the path to collective betterment.

Throughout my spiritual education, I was instructed to be more. In other words, I was to quiet my mind and find peace in doing nothing. This suggestion was difficult for me. I'm used to producing results, and in fact, I enjoy using my mind. So I have to be honest and say that I never appreciated the idea that my mind was not valued in my spiritual lessons and that I was continually told to stop doing and be – after all, I'm an American; I'm bred to do. Therefore, I only heeded their messages to a degree. Recognizing that I needed to still my mind more frequently in an effort to achieve greater personal balance, I also realized my mind's needs for purposeful actions and making a difference in the world, which made me feel like a worthwhile spirit.

The mind is very much a terrible thing to waste. In 2011 at age sixteen, a Dutch high school student decided to use his intellect to clean the oceans. Boyan Slat founded the Ocean Cleanup project after diving in Greece amid more trash than fish. Realizing the severity of our environmental disregard for the ocean's global impacts on all living beings, Slat set his mind toward finding a solution to one of humanity's gravest issues.

Over the last several years, Slat developed a system using solar powered trash-collecting booms, which launched late summer 2018, expecting to clean up 50% of the plastic and other wastes in the Pacific Ocean in just five years. In an article in Mother Nature Network, Boyan said, "I finally decided to put both university and my social life on hold to focus all my time on developing this idea. I wasn't sure if it would succeed, but considering the scale of the problem I thought it was important to at least try." Not only is Boyan's idea a success, but it's also sparking a rising tide of revolutionary thinking. However, his ingenious prowess would never have been realized if he hadn't been present and using his mind to actively assert his healing ideals in the world.

In our culture, we gear ourselves toward productivity, not contemplation. Yet rather than thinking there is something wrong with that ideal, perhaps we should understand the higher benefit of our cultural programming. Sitting in silence and holding your energy at an enlightened vibration brings balance to yourself, good energy to the world, and is absolutely a necessary practice. However, taking enlightened actions toward resolving our most pressing social, philosophical, and political life issues is also a necessity if we wish to heal the earth and all her inhabitants.

If you want to initiate higher transformation on the planet, embody your dreams and contribute to the higher ideals of others. Follow your unique cycle between being and doing, always remembering that one of the keys to mending the world is to use your ability to be present so that you can assist in the tangible advancement of yourself and humanity.

Alter Perspectives to Find Purpose in Your Circumstances

"Love is the absence of judgment."

– Dalai Lama, Tibetan Master

RENEE WAS IN A relationship with a married woman. While she believed her lover's promises that she would someday leave her wife, three years had passed with no end in sight. Renee started punishing herself with thoughts of guilt, dishonor and discouragement. She came to me needing insight as to why she still wholeheartedly believed she should wait for this woman, despite the unfair treatment to all parties involved. Given the nature of our session, I suggested that I perceive and Renee receive the information using one of my favorite intuitive tools: assuming the higher stance of neutrality and amusement.

One of the biggest life lessons that intuitive work has taught me is that there is truly no such thing as right or wrong; there is only experience and life lessons. For Renee and me to seek an intuitive understanding and solution to her relationship dilemma, we would need to be neutral and amused. This energetic stance would keep us out of judgment about the seemingly taboo and inappropriate subject of infidelity while allowing us to find the greater lesson so that Renee could grow into a greater love.

As I witnessed Renee's energy, I noticed that she carried the fear of trusting others. I could hear Renee's thoughts saying, "I can never count on love" and "Love never lasts." As I relayed this to Renee, she laughed and said that sounded like her. Love had let her down in childhood, and it continued into her adulthood. Unfortunately, her non-serving beliefs were attracting exactly what she didn't want.

Because Renee's thoughts were of disconnect and distrust, she was inadvertently creating a non-reciprocal relationship that mirrored her negative beliefs. With this understanding, Renee stopped judging herself for what she had perceived as "bad behavior." Instead, she began to learn from the situation and started to shift her beliefs about love, which eventually allowed her to release her attachment and grow beyond her limiting affair.

Everything happens for a reason, and no higher authority is condemning your choices nor sentencing you to a certain fate. There is only your perception of what is taking place in your life. Can you be neutral to your circumstances? Can you remain amused and aware of the situations holding you back so that you can grow beyond them? Let's explore your neutrality and amusement so that you can find the higher purpose in all your life's events.

Find Neutrality and Amusement

When you intuitively explore your life's dynamics, you may not always like what you see about either yourself or your situations. Thankfully, you can hold yourself in a state of neutrality and amusement to find the beauty in all your experiences. In this exploration, you will use the intuitive tool known as your halo or crown in order to enact your higher sense of objectivity. Earlier you placed a color that represented your sense of authority into your halo. You will now work further with this concept.

Your halo rests just above your head. Similar to your boundaries, your crown symbolically serves as another filter, allowing you to choose how you wish to perceive your life events. In other words, setting your halo to fear and defensiveness will cause you to perceive your circumstances as terrible, unfulfilling and cruel. However, viewing your life's situations with a crown of understanding and acceptance will invoke your peace of mind, allowing you to view events as meaningful. Try the intuitive practices below to explore and establish your neutrality and amusement.

1. Take a deep breath, close your eyes and imagine a halo spinning above your head.

2. Once you have a halo above you, imagine it to be the color orange. When your halo is set to orange, take a moment and intuit how this color makes you feel. Is it comfortable, or does it make you anxious? Remember, there is no wrong answer. However orange feels to you is correct.

3. Now move to another color. Change your halo to emerald green. Notice how you feel and how your energy shifts when you have your halo set to this color. Take a moment and intuit how emerald green affects you and your space.

4. Now set your halo to the color sky blue and notice what shifts. How does this color affect you versus all the other colors?

5. When you have completed this exercise in discerning different perspectives from the entire spectrum of colors, pick your unique color that represents neutrality to you. Set your crown to that hue and notice what happens to your space. You can always change this essence later, but for now, get a sense of perceiving your reality from the position of neutrality.

6. Yet it's not enough to be neutral. You also want to be amused as this element brings uplifting with understanding. Go ahead and find the color that represents amusement to you. Place that hue in your crown and notice the affect it has on you.

7. Now let's take this tool a step further and layer the energies of neutrality and amusement in your halo. Get a sense for how these

energies work together and how that can positively influence your life circumstances and relationships.

8. When you are done, you can leave your crown at neutrality and amusement or change it to anything you like. Sometimes when my day is complete, I will put my crown to the color of peace.

When you finish this exercise, reflect on what you noticed about using this skill. Ask yourself a few questions to ingrain these concepts:

- How did my energy feel and shift when my halo was set to orange? How might that affect my relationships and life circumstances?
- How did my energy feel and shift when my halo was set to emerald green? How does this affect my reality?
- How did my energy feel and shift when my halo was set to sky blue? How would this color affect my everyday life?
- What color did I use for neutrality? Why?
- How did my energy feel and shift when my halo was set to neutrality? What advantage does that give me?
- What color did I use for amusement? Why?
- How did my energy feel and shift when my halo was set to amusement? What advantages does amusement provide me in life?
- How did my energy shift when I set my halo to both neutrality and amusement? Where might this technique be valuable in my life?
- What energy did I put in my halo at the end of my exploration? Why? What will it do for me now?

Maintain Your Neutrality and Amusement

I have a hard time staying out of judgment while driving these days. It seems that everyone has moved to Colorado, and the increase in traffic is becoming unbearable, especially for a country girl like me. As a result, I often find myself judging the way other people drive and getting upset when they do something I think they shouldn't, like follow too closely or go too slowly.

Except the other day I was running late getting to my office, and in my rush, I cut off another driver. He angrily honked at me, and I felt bad but also had to laugh at myself. I realized that I was like everyone else. I, too, had moments when my driving was less than exemplary. In that moment, I vowed to always set my halo to neutrality and amusement when driving so that I could remain calm and accepting while on the roads.

You will want to develop and sustain your neutrality and amusement as a way of finding balance in all your life circumstances. Below is a simple intuitive practice you can use to expand and develop your ability to find the beauty in all your life's designs.

1. Thankfully, this is an easy tool to maintain. All you have to do is check in with your crown throughout the day to know what stance it is projecting. Remember that you don't always have to be in the place of neutrality and amusement. While those energies are best when you want to witness your energy or the energy of another, play with using other energies, such as enthusiasm, joy or passion, to match your present circumstances and the type of experiences you'd like to create in the moment.

Evolve Your Thinking

Of course, the last step in mastering this concept of neutrality and amusement is to consider the thoughts you have about these ideals. For instance, isolate the thoughts within you that sound like this: "There is a right way and wrong way of being," "There is nothing good in life," or "I have to be perfect and cannot make a mistake." Change those thoughts to match your higher understandings. As always, you can insert the following higher ideals or create some that work best for you.

"Everything I do is right and has purpose."

"Each person has a right to what is correct for them."

"There is beauty in every circumstance, as all our events are designed to help us grow."

Be Neutral to Others and Create a World of Acceptance and Peace

In the story of Renee and her participation in an extra-marital affair, neutrality allows us to refrain from judging the event. By remaining unbiased to the idea of infidelity, we find the higher purpose for her circumstances, discovering the growth her spirit planned for itself in order to heal her broken relationship ideals. In that sense, her culturally perceived inappropriate behavior was exactly what she needed to experience in order to learn how to shift her limiting beliefs about love. In that sense, how could Renee's actions be wrong?

There is never a truly right or wrong action, as all our deeds lead us to our evolution. One of the keys to promoting peace in the world requires that you recognize that people have a right to their unique expressions so that they can learn how to grow.

Interestingly, when you find objectivity and higher understanding regarding your personal life circumstances, a natural repercussion occurs that instantly creates a more loving planet. When you have more acceptance for yourself, you have more tolerance for others. One of the trends creating world change today is offering others the benefit of impartiality, breeding less societal expectation and more understanding and common ground.

As you conclude this chapter, you have gained all the knowledge and tools you need in order to be your own master. You have found the secret to taking responsibility for your circumstances, have discovered new solutions to overcoming your limited programming and life challenges, and you understand how to use your intuition to create positive change in the world. Yet it's important to note that you have also learned the customary foundations by which you will now approach your intuitive explorations.

As you move into parts four and five, each time you conduct an intuitive exercise, you will be using what you can consider the "Standard Preparation for All Your Intuitive Explorations," which consists of the skills you learned in the first half of this book. In an effort to help streamline this knowledge, you will find a reference section in the back, which combines the previous tools into one cohesive and easy to follow exercise. You can explore this reference now or anytime you wish to refresh your energy or discovery an intuitive truth. However, you will be prompted to follow these standards prior to exploring the rest of the concepts covered in this book.

With all the above in mind, your next step is to recognize how to use your intuition to maintain your four vital life foundations of mind, body, emotion and spirit found within your energetic field, so that you can heal yourself and bring greater awareness and innovation to all.

INTUITIVELY YOU

Restore Your Foundations and Create Healthy Communities

"The doctor of the future will be one's self."

– Albert Schweitzer, Nobel Prize Winning Physician and Philosopher

I FIRST MET Ethan when I interviewed him on my radio program. Ethan had a brilliant mind, having written numerous books about the ancient world's creation myths and beliefs about the origins of humanity. He had a wonderfully vast array of information that seemed to coincide with my own universal understandings, and it was easy for Ethan and me to become great friends. Unfortunately, Ethan suffered from severe depression. In the end, his inability to free himself from his debilitating disease would cause Ethan to lose his marriage, his career and, eventually, his life.

It would seem that while several industry leaders had published Ethan's work, academic scholars would not recognize his theories as valid. The higher institutions saw his research as independent, as it was not associated with a major university, and therefore unaccredited. Consequently, he spent countless hours in chat rooms vehemently defending his hypotheses with educators who would never give him his due. Ethan's wife once described how heated the online exchanges would become with objects being hurled about the house and Ethan stewing in anger for weeks following.

Over the years, Ethan's need to vindicate his work resulted in a tendency toward alcoholism, brooding and emotional distancing. Eventually, his wife divorced him, but not before the couple experienced financial ruin, as no press would publish Ethan's work due to his surly attitude. Seeking an answer to his plaguing life issues, Ethan once asked me what I thought he could do to change his fate.

As I intuitively witnessed Ethan's energy, I first noticed that his body and mind were out of alignment with his spirit and emotions. In other words, it seemed to me that Ethan was spending too much time trying to appease his ego and was not applying enough effort to following his heart. I then asked Ethan if there were endeavors he would like to pursue that didn't have anything to do with higher institutions and the need for their approval. Without hesitation, Ethan began describing a creative writing project he was thinking of producing. Suddenly, Ethan's entire countenance shifted from sullen and dejected to upbeat and excited as he shared his new idea with me.

The book was unlike anything Ethan had published in the past, as it was a science fiction novel based on a character similar to himself. It was an intricate notion with plenty of room for growth. I suggested that Ethan consider refocusing his work as a way of releasing his sadness and invoking more joy in his life. Instead of writing heady research theories, he could become a fiction author relaying fabulous tales of worlds that no one could tell him didn't exist.

Ethan loved the idea of becoming a science fiction author and for the first time in months seemed genuinely happy. He'd discovered a path that could lead him to fulfillment. Unfortunately, his ego would reestablish its reign, leaving his heart's work unrealized.

Try as he might, Ethan simply could not let go of his need to debate the academic authorities. Whenever someone contradicted his theories, he would engage in the negative loop, causing him to once again spiral into anger and despair. As a result, his novel idea was pushed aside, never being brought to life.

I hadn't spoken with Ethan in many months. Then one day, I received a most unexpected call from a friend informing me that Ethan had suddenly died of bladder cancer. I was shocked. I had no idea he was sick and couldn't believe he was gone. My only comforting thought was that he would not have to endure his torturous patterns any longer – except I couldn't help but wonder if his negative behaviors and self-denial weren't the real source of his disease.

In Louise Hay's book, *Heal Your Body: the Mental Causes for Physical Illness and the Metaphysical Way to Overcome* Them, she equates the anatomy of the body with the thoughts that can make it sick. In her work, Hay describes bladder problems occurring due to negative thoughts associated with anxiety, holding on to old ideas, fears of letting go, and being pissed off – all the behaviors Ethan had mastered. Interestingly, Hay also suggests replacing those thoughts with ideals that create healthier experiences such as, "I comfortably and easily release the old and welcome the new. I am safe." In other words, all the thoughts Ethan could not embrace. It made me question: If Ethan had shifted his focus from his mental pursuits of theory and research to his spiritual passion of imagination and story, would his body have needed to show him where he was in resistance to his higher evolution?

That you have a physical and mental body is tangible and obvious. However, less apparent is your etheric emotional and spiritual bodies, something most people never consider but which have serious implications on the quality of your life. Your four vital life foundations of spirit, emotions, mind and body combine to create your reality, with each requiring its own special attention in order to maintain one's overall health. You can think of it like this:

- Your spirit supports your free will and your ability to access universal knowledge, inspiration, potentiality and opportunity so that you can live your most idyllic reality.

- Your emotions support your ability to relate to yourself and others, as well as your ability to magnetize to yourself the elements necessary for creating your experiences.

- Your mind supports your cognitive reasoning and your ability to build systems around your spirit's potentials and desires.

- Your body supports your physical health and your tangible environment, embodying your higher intelligence and creating the material world around you.

In order to maintain good health, endearing relationships, financial stability, and a higher sense of purpose, each of our four vital life foundations must be in relative balance. In this section, you will learn to use your intuition to stabilize and sustain your fundamental bases so that you can achieve optimal health. Yet what I find most interesting about attaining personal balance is how it naturally makes you aware of the elements necessary for evolving our collective systems such as healthcare, education, politics and religion, ensuring that everyone experiences healthier life circumstances.

Maintain Physical Well-being and Cure the Healthcare Crisis

"Your body is a temple, but only if you treat it as one."

– Astrid Alauda, Author

GWEN HAD BEEN a client and student of mine for many years. Wanting a refresher on the basic intuitive tools, she decided to attend one of my beginner intuitive-development workshops. Part of what I teach new students is how to balance their foundations for increased well-being. By interpreting the symbolism in their energetic fields, students can determine the health of their foundational inner dynamics, get to the root cause of the areas of their life that need healing, and find solutions that bring more balance.

This concept of looking at the physical body through symbolism wasn't new to Gwen. I didn't think she would discover information she didn't already know. Yet while I was instructing the class to witness an animal that represented the state of their physical bodies, I could see Gwen nervously fidgeting, as if she was experiencing something she hadn't expected. Upon finishing the exploration, I asked if anyone wanted to share what he or she discovered. Gwen quickly threw her hand into the air and said, "I can't believe what I saw."

Gwen said that she had sensed a mouse as the symbolic representation of her physical health. Wanting anything but a mouse to be her animal message, Gwen tried to remove the symbol and start over. Unfortunately, the mouse was as persistent as mice generally are, and the image wouldn't go away. It was then that Gwen realized she was going to have to understand what the mouse was implying about her physical self, regardless of her resistance.

As she clairvoyantly observed the mouse, Gwen noticed it was limping. It occurred to her that the mouse had narrowly escaped a trap but had injured its right front leg beyond repair. More importantly, upon observing the scene, Gwen had an "aha" moment and finally understood the mouse's timely communication. Suddenly, she couldn't have been happier that the pesky critter had appeared.

Gwen had been experiencing a recurring shoulder injury that wasn't getting better. When she noticed that the mouse was injured, she immediately felt a pain in her right shoulder. Claircognizantly she knew that the critter was symbolically suggesting she seek a physician's diagnosis, as her pain was likely the indicator of a more serious issue. Gwen said that she had known that something was wrong with her arm but had been ignoring it. She felt that the mouse was telling her not to waste any more time. The next day, Gwen promptly made an appointment with her doctor. Much to her astonishment, it was later determined that she had developed advanced degeneration in the joint and would need surgery.

Gwen's story demonstrates how your intuition can provide insight into your physical health issues even prior to seeing a doctor. Think of the money, time and hassles you could save with your intuitive advanced-warning system aiding you on your journey to greater health. Let's observe your physical health now so that your body can experience greater vitality.

Explore Your Physical Health

Exploring physical health is one of my favorite intuitive tools. Who doesn't love animals, either up close or from afar? However, what I most enjoy about this exploration is how profound it can be. Though I never know what animal is going to show up, it is always on point and directly related to something I'm experiencing physically, whether minor or major. Follow the intuitive steps outlined below to discover the state of your tangible self.

1. Start by following the Standard Preparation for All Intuitive Explorations found as in the reference section in the back of this book.

2. When you have completed the steps in the preparation, begin your discovery by intuitively asking to witness an animal on your screen that represents the current state of your physical health. This could take a moment – be patient. Also, be sure to use all your cornerstone instincts of clairvoyance, clairaudience, clairsentience, and claircognizance to see, hear, sense and simply know what animal is showing up.

3. Once you see a figure, take your time to use your senses to observe, listen and feel the animal's behaviors and attitudes. You can even take note of the environment in which you witness your critter.

Once you have observed your physical body's symbolism, ask yourself a few questions in order to gain a better understanding of what this animal messenger is telling you about your physical well-being and its needs.

- What animal represented the current state of my physical self?
- What attitude did my animal assume? Why?
- How did the animal react to its environment? Why?
- What does this animal and its behaviors tell me about the state of my physical health?
- What can I do to achieve improved physical health?

- How does this information help me to achieve greater balance?

Maintain Your Physical Health

For many years, Candice thought that she was developing diabetes. She had many of the symptoms and often felt the need to eat better and exercise more. However, Candice was young and didn't want to be bothered with what she perceived as restrictions and so she ignored her inner promptings in lieu of fun decadence and overdoing.

Then one day, ten years down the road, Candice got her wake up call. She had diabetes. Suddenly, all the food in her kitchen cupboards was off limits, and her daily activities would need to change drastically. Feeling overwhelmed, she quickly started to educate herself on the topic. Which type of insulin was best for her? Which types of foods should she eat? How much exercise did she need? With her newfound knowledge, she began to change her lifestyle. However, try as she might, her fresh diet and aggressive fitness regime was proving harder to maintain than she anticipated. Within a few weeks, she was back to her old habits.

Over the next three months, Candice's health would severely decline. At one point, she even had a hyperglycemic episode and needed hospitalization. It seemed to Candice that she was going to have to learn to be dedicated to a new lifestyle if she wanted to live at all.

Maintaining your physical health can be a challenge; however, your body is always telling you what it needs to be healthy. As you gain an understanding of how your intuition works to alert you to your physical well-being, you will want to give your body what it needs in that moment so that you can experience all the best that life has to offer for years to come. This may very well require you to incorporate more activity and healthy foods into your routines. Be willing to rise to the challenge, as your new habits will elevate your spirit and provide you access to greater health and more enjoyable experiences. Here are a few ways you can maintain your body's needs:

1. Regularly find the animal that best represents your physical body in any moment, whether you feel ill or not. Being aware of your body's baseline is a great way to know if and when it shifts into an unhealthy state.

2. Take action toward what your body wants through diet, exercise, stillness and intuitive exploration. However, be wary not to interpret your body's messages as the need to be pencil-thin or ultra-fit. Remember, part of the higher-minded changes taking place today include full-size models in advertising because, let's face it, we are full-size people. Activity and diet can be healthy and uplifting, but if you are obsessive about achieving a look, you are feeding your ego and not your body. Find your unique personal balance, not the balance you believe a cultural or social construct would have you adopt.

Evolve Your Thinking

Of course, you will also need to monitor the thoughts you have about your physical being in order to manifest greater physical health. Unfortunately, most people's thoughts about their bodies are some of the lowest thoughts we can have and, therefore, are the hardest to retrain.

In a culture that values looks over mind, youth over wisdom, and status and power over everything, the ideas we have about maintaining our physical appearances can be unrealistic and depressing, which never leads to increased health. At some point, you have to be real with yourself and change your programmed beliefs about what the right body is for you. You can start by finding the thoughts within you that resemble these: "I'm ugly," "My body is unhealthy," or "I have to be the size of a waif, own a hotel, and date a famous sports figure to be somebody." When you've identified your negative self-talk, shift those thoughts to supportive ideas like the ones below or, as always, design your own.

"Beauty is energetic."

"I love my body and want to treat it well."

"My body has its own idea about the shape it wants to be."

Intuition's Role in Transforming the American Healthcare System

One of the biggest American dilemmas we face is how to develop healthcare structures that adequately accommodate the needs of all but don't break the bank. However, perhaps the reason we are having such a difficult time figuring out how best to manage our systems is that we are approaching the issue with only half the equation.

Western medicine only treats the body and mind. It does not recognize how spirit and emotions influence one's total health. Yet as Ethan's story demonstrated, your spirit vitally needs your attention. Therefore, if the healthcare industry really wants to aid people in healing, it will gain knowledge of the science of one's spirit and emotions so that they are working with a person's totality and not just half a picture. It should be mandatory for healing professionals to receive education on using intuition to discern one's energy anatomy, as insight is the ultimate healing component.

However, the first step toward fixing our healthcare crisis is not to rely on the system to take care of us but to use our intuition to manage our personal health as a form of preventative care. Remember Candice and her need for hospitalization? Her unwillingness to be responsible for her personal health resulted in her incurring thousands of dollars in unnecessary medical bills. Moreover, she put additional strain on the hospital's doctors and nurses, taking time away from patients truly in need.

If Candice had adhered to her intuition by eating properly and getting routine exercise, the medical resources she absorbed could have gone toward nobler efforts such as eradicating disease and providing universal healthcare to all. Instead, her insurance premiums skyrocketed, and she needed to incorporate yet another expensive medicine into her budget.

One of the ways in which you can personally assist the healthcare system is to use your intuition as a preventative tool against emotional, mental, spiritual and physical disease. If you intuitively discover that you have an emotional block from a past disappointment, you can release the emotion, freeing yourself from the dynamic, or you can hold on to your wounding, like Ethan, allowing it to fester until it becomes a clog in your physical being. Either way, you are accountable for the health your choice creates.

It is your job to manage your healthcare long before it is an institution's responsibility. Just as going to the dentist for a cleaning is a defense against cavities and the cost of repairing them, conducting intuitive checkups on your four vital life foundations can avert unnecessary pain as well as avoid drains on your personal finances and the collective resources of our social systems.

There is a shift taking place in our collective thinking about what type of healthcare we truly require. Individuals are becoming increasingly aware of the negative health benefits of additives, sugars, hormones, dyes and other unnatural ingredients in their food. They are also becoming aware of the terribly addictive side effects that certain pharmaceuticals can create, wreaking havoc in our lives. Furthermore, they've watched enough Oprah to know that they have a mind, body and soul that must be considered in the healing equation. Consequently, people are seeking a more integrated and holistic style of healthcare that includes higher-minded and energetic-alternative practices of healing, such as reiki, ayurvedic medicine, holistic nutrition, intuitive therapy, meridian tapping, shamanic journeying, and life coaching, just to name a few.

You can help form this growing trend of integrative and holistic healthcare by first listening to your intuition and following its higher suggestions regarding your body and its well-being. You can also start seeking alternative views in conjunction with your Western approaches so you can discover your unique healing while helping the collective move toward a more expanded perspective of universal healthcare.

Maintain Mental Health and Find a New Public Education

"The pendulum of the mind oscillates between sense and nonsense, not between right and wrong."

– Carl Jung, Swiss psychiatrist

PAIGE WAS A daughter, wife and mother, but more than anything, Paige was a worrier. She was obsessively concerned about her husband, children and parents. She worried that her spouse wasn't eating properly or getting enough rest, fretted over the safety of her children, and fussed excessively over her parents as if they knew nothing of the ways of the world.

However, as often happens in cases of disproportionate concern, Paige developed a compulsive anxiety disorder. Consequently, she took pharmaceuticals to control her heart palpitations and mood swings. She even started seeing a counselor and took up meditating to alleviate her fears. Yet while Paige was following the advice of her doctors, she wasn't finding the relief she sought. The medications were making her lethargic, deep breathing only relieved her anxiety for a few moments, and talking about her fears seemed to make them more real and even worse.

I met Paige when she decided to explore alternatives to curing her anxiety and enrolled in my intuitive development workshop. Paige wasn't new to meditation, but she was new to intuitive exploration and had no idea whether or not it would help her lessen her concerns. However, when I instructed the students to explore a house that symbolically represented the state of their mental health, Paige began to understand how to rid herself of fretfulness and all its pills.

After the exercise, Paige described her metaphorical house as being made of exceptionally fragile glass. She said she was certain it was going to shatter at any moment and was making her restless and anxious. However, when I suggested that the students also notice the surroundings of their internal home, Paige said her glass house was positioned next to her current place of residence. She could even see her family members playing and having fun in the backyard. While Paige's symbolic residence of mental health was frail, the house beside her, where her loved ones resided, was strong, rooted, and could stand the test of time.

Paige was surprised. She had never witnessed the reality her mind was creating from this perspective and could finally see what she was doing to herself and how it was keeping her from being in the same place as her family. Yet, it wasn't until Paige noticed a storm over her glass home that she received the intuitive solution to end her worry.

During the exercise, I instructed the students to notice the weather surrounding their symbolic house. It was then that Paige noticed a dark storm looming over the top of her mental abode and feared that it might hail on the delicate structure. However, when Paige looked to see if the storm was over her family's house, she noticed that the weather there was calm, sunny and, more importantly, unthreatened by any ominous disaster.

I asked Paige what she thought her intuitive impression might be telling her about her mental behaviors and the effects they were having on her reality. Without hesitation, she said, "Obviously, I'm far too serious, which is causing me to be overly obsessive and fearful of turmoil."

Paige explained that she had grown up with the belief that life is serious, and when you become an adult, you give up childish things in lieu of responsibility. As a result, Paige's mind forgot how to be innocent and developed an overly somber attitude. Unfortunately, her belief that adults can't have fun was causing her to presume the worst and to take every measure to avoid a potential catastrophe no matter how unrealistic.

I then asked Paige what her glass house needed in order to lessen its worries and obsessions. Paige's eyes filled with tears of relief, as she had just found the cure for her anxiety. "It needs to shatter, to be destroyed and I need to be in my family's home, where everyone is safe and I can learn to play again."

Even more profound, when I asked Paige what effect changing her core beliefs and patterns about the roles of adults would have in her life, she smirked and said, "Besides connecting more with my family, I'd likely stop binge eating and lose fifty pounds." The class laughed with Paige and her ability to make fun of the situation, but we all understood the depth of truth in her words. In the end, Paige's decision to let go of her fragile mental construct and find more time for play created the balance she was seeking.

Your mind is a powerful generator aiding you in building your ideal circumstances. Let's explore your mental health now so that you are aware of where your mind resides and what it needs to establish peace.

Explore Your Mental Health

Are you curious about where your mental body resides? I can tell you that my mental body lives in many different places depending on my circumstances. My etheric house can exist in a desert and be devoid of furnishings during times when I feel unsupported. My residence might even be positioned in an overly crowded city and be littered with clutter at times when I'm overwhelmed or frustrated. My state of mind can even dwell in a lush garden with a soft breeze blowing through it when I'm with my partner having deep and meaningful discussions. The steps below will aid you in witnessing a house that represents the state of your current mental health so that you can consider what you might need in order to achieve the balance you desire.

1. You will want to start by following the Standard Preparation for All Intuitive Explorations found as a reference in back.

2. When you have completed the steps in the preparation, begin your discovery by using your clairvoyance, clairaudience, clairsentience and claircognizance and asking to observe a house on your screen that represents your mental self and health.

3. Take a moment to notice the details of your house. Notice the exterior condition of your home and its foundation.

4. Next witness the interior of your home, taking note of the state of the inside of your home.

5. Lastly, pay attention to the surrounding environment in which your house resides. Notice the weather surrounding your structure and the way it might affect the stability of your house.

Once you have intuitively witnessed your house, reflect on this experience by asking yourself the following questions:

- What was the condition of my house's exterior and foundation? What might that tell me about my current mental health?

- What was the condition of my house's interior and design? What might that tell me about my mind's well-being?

- Where was my residence? Did I have neighbors or was it isolated? What does that tell me about the state of my mind?

- What weather conditions were taking place around my home? How is that affecting my mental health?

- What can I do to achieve greater mental balance?

- How does witnessing the state of my mind's health help me in my everyday circumstances?

Maintain Your Mental Health

Mental health can be tricky to manage, which is why it's important that you clearly understand your mind's function, never expecting it to be something beyond its design. For years, I tried to think my way to increased health, wealth and well-being. Unfortunately, all I could come up with was more of the same – different job, same politics, new relationship, same insecurities. It wasn't until I understood that my mind was not responsible for generating ideas that I stopped relying on it to discover my solutions.

Your mind is not the place to conceive innovations and revelations – that's your spirit's job. Your mind can only work with what spirit brings to it as inspiration. In our culture, we place great emphasis on logic and the ability to compute and reason. We believe our minds to be our masters. Yet perhaps we should rethink that stance.

Albert Einstein is widely quoted as saying, "The intuitive mind is a sacred gift and the rational mind is a faithful servant. We have created a society that honors the servant and has forgotten the gift." He clearly understood that the mind does not come before the spirit. Rather, the mind is a by-product of your higher self 's desire to live a physical reality. If you want to achieve personal balance, you must reorient your perspective away from being the servant and toward being the master of your intuitive gifts.

The key to a balanced mind is not to put the burden of problem solving on it but to allow spirit to bring to your mind realizations and inspirations around which it can then develop structures and protocols. Therefore, maintaining good mental health means increasing your ability to be open to receiving your higher wisdom. Follow the steps below and discover how to create sustainable peace of mind.

1. To develop your mental health, first practice passive meditation, or what we think of as traditional meditation, where you sit for ten to twenty minutes and focus on nothing. This is great for releasing tension and resetting your behaviors.

2. You can also use breath as a means of clearing your mind. Sit quietly and take ten deep breaths slowly and methodically inhaling for a count of six to eight, and exhaling for a count of six to eight, allowing the rhythmic motion to release your thoughts. This

technique is actually harder to do than you might think. Give it a try and test your ability to focus.

3. You can also practice active meditation as a means of maintaining good mental health. Active meditation is contemplative and is done by lying down, sitting up or even walking while focusing on one issue, image, sensation or idea for the purpose of gaining intuitive understanding and healing. All the exercises in this book fall under this category. Embark on a meditative journey whenever you want to discover insights into your unique life issues.

4. Unless you are a Millennial, it's likely that you've forgotten how to play. Most adults have let this part of themselves go. However, play is a key element designed to rejuvenate and refresh your mind. The great thing about the idea of fun is that you can play at anything you like so long as it brings you joy. You can learn a musical instrument, take up golf, make jewelry, bake specialty pastries, go for a hike, or be outside with the kids kicking a ball and skipping rope. The point is that you don't have to wait until vacation to have fun. Have fun every day and let your inner child give your mind a break from its structured perceptions.

5. Also, one the greatest things the mind enjoys is building structure around what it knows. I like to give my mind creative projects that don't necessarily have to equate success, like organizing the house, uncovering family genealogy, or volunteering with a community effort. The purpose of giving my mind a chore is to give it something constructive with which to occupy itself so that it doesn't have excessive time to analyze and over think. Healthy distractions aid the mind in thinking outside its box as well as bringing it relief, purpose and connection.

6. I'm now going to say something that most spiritual teachers would not say. Ego is not bad. Now of course, you can be overly egotistical, which harms your spirit and the spirit of others, but ego, when used properly, can be motivating in ways that push you past your limitations and procrastinations. If you want to obtain a

coveted career position but are fearful of being outspoken or noticed in your job, your ego can aid you in feeling confident, worthy and empowered, helping you to move past your isolating fears so that you are recognized in your field. Don't demonize your ego; it serves a purpose. When it's appropriate, let it prop you up. Just remember to let it serve your higher ideals rather than run the show.

Evolve Your Thinking

The next step toward greater mental health is to retrain the thoughts that keep you limited. Those thoughts can sound similar to these. "I only trust my mind, not my emotions or spirit," "I never know the right things to do and should just do as I'm told," or "Fear, fear, fear." Remember to shift these thoughts to positive and supportive ideals. As usual you can use one of the mantras below or create your own.

"My mind is not in charge, but it is at my command."

"Every choice I make is right for me."

"Everything happens for a good reason; what is my lesson?"

Intuition's Role in Transforming the American Educational System

One of the biggest challenges that we as a nation face today is the reforming of our educational systems. Recent reports indicate that not only is violence much too prevalent in our schools but also our teaching methods are not advancing our children as predicted by school board administrators.

The Brookings Institute's 2018 report titled, 'How Well are American Students Learning?" states that test gaps in civics scores remain alarmingly wide, pointing out that, "Test score gaps by race, ethnicity, and family income remain distressingly wide, and although racial and ethnic gaps show signs of slow improvement, little in the recent trends suggests the gaps will close in the near future."

Other studies, such as the "Public Education Funding Inequity: In an Era of Increasing Concentration of Poverty and Resegregation," published in January 2018 by the U.S. Commission on Civil Rights, also suggest that our educational system is still acutely segregated and that many under-privileged classrooms lack skilled teachers, intensive curriculums, and adequate funding.

It was even found that in comparison to many other countries, the American educational system didn't fare well, although this statistic didn't seem to matter much, all things considered. Curiously, countries once thought to have mastered their public school systems, like Finland, New Zealand, France, and Germany, were also experiencing their own gaps and declines, performing no better than the U.S. in the long run. In other words, globally we are missing the mark and are failing to properly educate the future generations.

How could it be that with our first-world knowledge and technological advancements, we still have poorly funded and subpar programs for educating children? The answer is simple. We've reached the cap of what we can teach and learn by only using our minds. However, Americans have the opportunity to change our educational trend. We can set a new standard of learning by incorporating the intuitive sciences into our curriculums. This higher education would then demonstrate for the world how to foster healthy, free-thinking, and innovative people who not only take responsibly for themselves, but are also beholden to the earth and all her inhabitants.

The solution to aiding our youth in increasing their mental acuity, rising above poverty, and eradicating hatred begins by teaching them how to see life from a higher perspective. While it is important that individuals learn to read, write and calculate, it is more imperative that they learn to recognize their energetic environments so that they can achieve both inward and outward balance.

The bottom line is… intuition equals intelligence. One of the greatest things we can do to move with the rising tide of change is offer students as young as age six courses on intuition as a means of becoming personally empowered and collectively united.

Maintain Emotions and Resolve Political Divisiveness

"Let's not forget that the little emotions are the great captains of our lives and we obey them without realizing it."

– Vincent Van Gogh, Dutch painter

NADJA WAS THIRTY-FIVE the year she lost her mother to cancer, her father to heart failure, and her sister-in-law in a car accident. Nadja was devastated, thinking that the universe was conspiring against her, and fell into a deep depression. Five years and multitudes of antidepressants later, she was still unable to move beyond her sorrow. A friend of Nadja's suggested that she attend one of my intuitive development workshops in hopes that Nadja might find a way to alleviate the grief consuming her.

In the workshop, I instructed the class to look at a flower that represented their current emotional state and see what perspective it implied that they could shift to achieve greater balance. During the exploration, I noticed that Nadja was in tears. This is not unusual in a healing setting. In fact, I've often thought of calling this class "Epiphanies Are Us," as many students find life-changing solutions to their biggest challenges. Tears are a natural part of their relief and joy. However, Nadja's emotional awakening bordered on sobbing, which told me that she was experiencing something extraordinary. I quietly slipped a tissue into her hand and continued. When I concluded the exploration and asked if anyone wanted to share his or her experience, Nadja instantly raised her hand.

Nadja said that her emotional flower came to her as a giant sunflower that was seedless in the middle, wilting and dying. The picture was no surprise to her, as this was exactly how she had been feeling for the last five years. However, during the exploration, when I instructed the class to observe the surroundings of their flower, Nadja had an emotional breakthrough.

Nadja said that she had expected her emotional flower to be in a remote desert, isolated, far from any love, support or purpose, but what she found was quite the opposite. As Nadja intuitively witnessed the setting of her flower, she realized that she was in a field of sunflowers that were vibrant and thriving. Yet believing that couldn't be true, she tried to change the image to something more bleak. However, as is generally the case, the intuitive image was persistent, and she couldn't ignore the scene. Nadja then decided she would have to see what the depiction wanted her to know about healing her emotions.

As Nadja further inspected her environment, she noticed that three particularly larger sunflowers encircled her flower, seemingly watching over her and keeping her safe. Then, much to Nadja's surprise, clairaudiently she heard her mother's voice coming from one of the large sunflowers saying to her, "I've never left. Don't give up. There is much love in life for you still." At this point in Nadja's account, her tears truly became sobs along with the tears of many of us in class.

Nadja said that the unexpected nature of her experience had filled her with a validation and certainty that her mother, father and sister-in-law were happy and thriving in their new landscape. More importantly, Nadja finally understood that her family's energetic essences were still present and would always remain with her. In that moment, a dark veil lifted from Nadja as her emotions finally received the freedom and relief they needed, giving her new hope for love and happiness in her life.

Emotions are unpredictable. When a spirit makes a plan to have a physical experience, emotions are the factor it cannot account for, which can throw its design off track. When have your emotions gotten the better of you? Whether you experience loss or heartbreak or even triumph and elation, your emotions heighten and activate instinctive responses within you that you may not know how to control if you are unconscious of the bigger picture. The key is to be intuitively aware of your emotional condition so you don't shut down that part of you or overly activate it based on the reality of your situations. Let's discover the state of your emotional health now so that you discover greater personal balance.

Explore Your Emotional Health

The first time I explored the state of my emotions, I found nothing, which told me everything. When I was a child, the adults in my life did not tolerate emotions. My sister and I were discouraged from crying or laughing too loudly, and there certainly wasn't permission for complaining. As a result, my emotional essence was not evolving, which is why nothing appeared in my exploration. Realizing that my lack of emotional presence was the reason I was single, had no friends and felt isolated, I decided it was time to evolve my emotions.

Over a series of months, I focused all my attention on being clairsentient. As I went into a room, I would feel the energies rather than hearing them. When I was with clients, I concentrated on feeling their issues rather than seeing them. I even started expressing my emotions rather than stuffing them down. Interestingly, the repercussions of being more emotionally aware started a trend in which I was manifesting more business, greater health, and new friendships and was connecting more deeply with my partner. In this exploration, you can intuitively witness your current emotional health and the healing it might need in order to create your ideal reality.

1. To begin, follow the Standard Preparation for All Intuitive Explorations in the back of this book.
2. Once you have your energy set, start by using your clairvoyance, clairaudience, clairsentience or claircognizance and imagine on your viewing screen a flower that represents your emotional health. Be sure to notice the details of your flower.
3. Take note of the color, quality and texture of your flower. Smell the flower and attune to its unique vibration. Observe the leaves, stem and roots, gauging how your flower feels emotionally at this time.
4. Now, witness the landscape where your flower resides. Pay attention to its surroundings, the weather, and even what time of day it is, noting how this scene makes you feel.

Once you have witnessed your flower, discern what you learned about your emotional state by asking yourself a few questions:

- What did my flower look like? What was its color, quality, and texture, and how did this make me feel about my life circumstances?
- What was the condition of the leaves, stems, and roots? How do I feel about the foundations of my emotions?
- What were the setting and surroundings of my flower? Was I contented with this picture?
- Based on what I noticed with my flower, what shifts in my emotional perceptions can I make that better support my health and my life's desires and goals?
- How does witnessing the state of my emotions help me in my everyday circumstances?

Maintain Your Emotional Health

"When emotions are expressed...all systems are united and made whole. When emotions are repressed, denied, not allowed to be whatever they may be, our network pathways get blocked, stopping the flow of the vital feel-good, unifying chemicals that run both our biology and our behavior."

– Candace B. Pert, Molecules Of Emotion: The Science Behind Mind-Body Medicine

Candace Pert is a leading researcher in the field of energy medicine. She understands the importance your emotions play in generating your life's circumstances. When you hold back, deny or overly express your emotions, you create energy clogs that can eventually take the form of physical illness, as likely happened to Ethan.

Part of maintaining your emotional health requires a willingness to give proper attention to your feelings. Below are a few suggestions for how you can continue to become familiar with your emotions and how to apply your higher understanding in the world.

1. Express your emotions, but don't dwell on them. Specifically, don't dwell on negative emotions lest you manifest your fears. For example, overly obsessing about the feeling that you don't have enough money will cause you to not have money. Make sure you know the reality your emotions are creating. Think of it like this: Emotions are not truths; they are feelings designed to bring you to your truths. Express your emotions so that you know what you feel, then choose what you really believe and shift the emotion to match.

2. Practice sensing the emotions of others around you. If you are empathic and have a hard time detaching from other people's energy, remember to use boundaries and not take on another person's energy as your own. The point is to be open to feeling and getting used to sensing your environment this way but not living the emotions of others.

3. Lastly, don't be afraid to be vulnerable. Be willing to be more social and let people get to know you. Be willing to express your fears and excitement even if it feels childlike. Speak from your heart, withholding the need to manipulate or have an agenda for others. Use boundaries to protect yourself, but be open to the world with wonder and awe like a child, and trust that vulnerability will lighten your vibration, bringing you into alignment with a life in which you are able to connect more deeply with others and yourself.

Evolve Your Thinking

During this time of great shift, you will also want to monitor the thoughts you have about your emotions in order to bring them into balance. Discover the thoughts you have that say, "My problems are worse than anyone else's," "I'm a victim to my circumstances and have no control over life," or "The world is full of pain, and I can't bear it." Shift the thoughts into alignment with the times today. Below are some suggestions for how to change your thoughts, but of course, you can always create your own.

"Everyone faces challenges, and mine are no worse or better."

"I am the creator of my life and have designed all my experiences for growth."

"The world is in agreement with its circumstances, and I just have to be the best me possible and send love to everyone else."

Your Intuition's Ability to Transform Political Agendas

One of the most emotionally charged and divisive elements of American life is politics. You can't go to a Fourth of July barbeque without getting caught up in a political discussion about what truly does or doesn't make America great. Unfortunately, these debates generally result in anger, frustration, and ill will toward others because people cannot unanimously agree on politics – as if we are all supposed to think the same. We are not!

The problem with politics is not policy; it is that we use it to validate our lower thinking in hopes that someone will tell us we are correct. Because we do not recognize intuition and specifically our ability to be claircognizant, we do not trust and cannot find peace with our perceptions and decisions. As a result, we seek outside justification for our beliefs in hopes that someone will substantiate our ideals. Unfortunately, this need to be right causes us to deny all other opinions, because our egos get in the way.

While we can justify the need to educate others on topics we feel they are uninformed about, we have to stop short of needing them to concede to our beliefs and ideals. Thankfully, intuition allows us to draw that fine line, prompting us to state our opinions and perceived facts but then letting go of the need to control other people's responses. Remember, most of the time we speak only to hear ourselves so that we can determine our own beliefs. It doesn't matter what others accept as truth.

Lest we forget, a true Democracy accommodates both individual opinion and majority rule. What is right for one person can never be right for all. Just the fact that we have both the female and male personas on the planet tells us that we live in a world of opposites attracting, which is apparently the way it's supposed to be. We were not intended to be the same; rather we were meant to blend our differences to create higher ways of being. What do you think would happen if people stopped arguing for the sake of validating themselves and started offering acceptance to one another instead? Perhaps common ground wouldn't be so difficult to find.

There is no doubt that American politics resembles something of a three-ring circus these days with our 45th Commander in Chief acting as ringleader. Yet all things serve a purpose, and our political spectacle demonstrates what happens when Americans forget that they live in a democracy with the right to free speech and to elect what is in the best interest of all. However, there is another rising tide of change ensuing that government doesn't take precedence over people.

After the American President chose to pull out of the Paris Climate Change Accord, American individuals and businesses adamantly reaffirmed their continued commitment to uphold the values of the agreement. These people took it upon themselves to take right action without the need of our federal government's mandate or acknowledgement. The bottom line is that our lives don't have to change by the man or woman who's elected. WE THE PEOPLE are always in charge should we be willing to assert our higher ideals.

When it comes to politics in America, it's best to use your higher knowledge to set aside your need to be correct. Don't let your primal passions engage you in the fight for needless acknowledgement. Conduct your own independent research on the political issues and discuss opinions with others without needing to be right or wrong. Then use your intuition to discern the transparency of your candidates and exercise your inalienable right to vote for who will truly uphold your higher ideals. However, remember not to put the burden of change on your elected officials. Support and build businesses that uphold the greatest good for all, swaying the tide and changing the world without needing government approval.

Maintain Spiritual Health and Find Peace with All Beliefs

"A merry heart doeth good like a medicine, but a broken spirit dries the bones."

– Proverbs 17:22

VALERIE WAS A healing touch practitioner. She received an excellent education on energy anatomy and worked at a hospital assisting individuals in shifting the energies in their fields so that they could experience increased health. Valerie found herself drawn to this type of work in part due to its quiet nature, which she believed matched her own. Healing touch is a type of energy work achieved in a meditative manner with silence. Unfortunately, Valerie's peaceful workplace had become anything but calm, challenging her sensibilities.

Valerie noticed she was experiencing strange events when working with patients. While her external setting was soothing, allowing her clients to fall into a deep stillness, Valerie's internal world was running amok. She found herself flooded with images, sounds and feelings about her clients' health, which she had no idea how to handle. Interestingly, this type of energetic bombardment is the plight of most, if not all, alternative practitioners as well as many massage therapists, nurses, social workers, teachers, and even hair stylists – really anyone who works with others physically or through counseling. So yes, bartenders, baristas, and even sales persons often receive insights for others. The problem is that we don't have an understanding of our intuition, let alone how and why it provides information.

Valerie's five years of extensive education on energy and healing had never once covered the subject of intuition and its ability to perceive healing insight. It occurred to me that even our holistic healing programs might be missing the mark by not including the vital element of intuition in healthcare. Thankfully, Valerie took it upon herself to get her intuitive education by attending classes. Much to her joy, she would find a solution to her psychic dilemma that would open up new avenues of work and fulfillment for her.

Valerie was attending a workshop in which I had students witness the state of their spirits. Just as you've witnessed your body, mind and emotions, I asked the students to discover the color that best represented their spirit in the present moment. Valerie described the color of her spirit as a mesmerizing electric blue. Valerie also noticed that there were other beams of light attracted to her energy. I asked Valerie what she thought this image was telling her about the state of her spirit, and she said, "I think my spirit is exceptionally bright and full of knowledge. I believe other spirits, like my patients, come to me for help in expressing what their own spirits need to say."

Brilliant, I thought. Valerie had never seen herself as a bright light with much to offer. Suddenly, she had a more empowered sense of herself. I then asked Valerie if she thought that was a healthy dynamic for her, or if she wanted to change this element. With much excitement, Valerie said she didn't want to change a thing and, instead, wanted to expand it further. Valerie felt a sense of purpose at the prospect of being able to intuitively aid other individuals.

Then all of a sudden, Valerie's enthusiasm waned as she remembered that she worked in a hospital that did not allow her to offer intuitive information to her clients. I reassured Valerie that she didn't need to worry, as she had other options. I suggested that she consider enrolling in my Intuitive Practitioner Program as a way to hone her higher senses and learn the ethics and business of using intuition as a therapy. The course would teach her how to start a private healing practice, offering her insights to clients outside the hospital setting.

Valerie followed my advice and eventually began offering her insights as a second job. Interestingly, Valerie felt that her clients were experiencing greater healing results when she included her intuitive interpretations, as this helped them get to the root cause of their issues. She was thrilled with the direction of her career and the sense that she was truly making a difference.

Have you ever thought of yourself as a spirit with access to other people's healing information as well as your own? Furthermore, are you aware of the potentials and possibilities your spirit can provide you? Your spirit is always accessing universal wisdom and healing that you can use for yourself or impart to others as a means of creating greater balance. If you don't pay attention to the messages you receive from your spirit, you will likely miss your personal life solutions and opportunities and won't be able to help others find theirs either.

Explore Your Spiritual Health

Your spirit is responsible for planning the direction of your life. Your spirit designs a life based on the type of growth it needs. When you can intuitively interact with your higher self, you find your life's purpose and plan. In this exploration, you will witness the color that represents the state of your current spiritual health. As you view your color, you will be receiving information about your current state of etheric health.

1. As per the usual, start by following the Standard Preparation for All Intuitive Explorations located in the reference section.
2. When you are done with your preparation, use all your senses to see, hear, feel and know to help you witness the color of your spirit on your screen. Be sure to give extra attention to the depth, clarity and texture of your spirit's color.

After witnessing the color of your spirit, take a moment and ask yourself questions about your spirit so that you can achieve greater awareness.

- What color, clarity, quality and texture was my spirit?
- What about my spirit color appealed to me? Why and what does that tell me about my spiritual well-being?
- What did not appeal to me about the color of my spirit? Why? What does that tell me about the state of my spiritual self?
- What does my spirit want that is not being creating in my life?
- How does witnessing the state of my emotional health help me in my everyday circumstances?

Maintain Your Spiritual Health

Your spirit is always speaking to you, and so are the spirits of other people. I recall once having a strange realization about how spirit reaches out to us. While I was running errands one day, I kept noticing random women who looked like my best friend from high school. These people were obviously not my childhood friend, but I kept seeing them and thinking of her. I hadn't thought about my friend in many years, as our lives took different directions. I wondered why I was suddenly seeing her in others. Much to my amazement, later that night I noticed that I had a Facebook friend request from my childhood schoolmate. That's when I realized that I had been seeing her around town because her spirit was in search of me.

Spirit shows up in nature and through other people, as well as in the form of your inner guidance. Develop your spiritual balance so that you can be privy to spirit's influence in your life.

1. Reading this book and intentionally using your intuition in everyday life are two of the best things you can do to improve your unique spiritual connections and subsequent health. You can also support

your spiritual health by recognizing that you are spirit before body and that your truth is the only truth that matters.

2. Another great way to foster your spiritual health is to honor your personal timing. Your spirit naturally stays in flow with the energetic cycles of time. In other words, if the cycle is poised for a particular activity or for productivity, your spirit will feel energized and eager to get at it. However, if the cycle is right for you to rest and reassess, your spirit will be still and contemplative. Follow your personal timing, and resist forcing your mind's agenda. Simply pay attention to your spirit's needs, not controlling it but allowing life to flow with greater ease.

Evolve Your Thinking

After assessing the state of your spiritual being, be sure to find any of the negative thoughts you have about being a spirit, and retrain those thoughts so that your ideals match your newfound understandings. Listen for the voice in you that says, "I have no power over my experiences," "I never have good ideas," or "I can't express what I really believe." Shift those thoughts toward more empowering statements such as the ones listed below, or develop your own supportive mantras.

"I am an all-powerful spiritual being."

"My spirit brings me insight and inspiration."

"My spirit is free to express itself."

Intuition's Role in Transforming our Cultural Belief Systems

As a girl, I attended a Baptist church. While I loved Sunday school with the activities it provided, such as making crosses out of gold colored macaroni, when I got older and it was time to attend adult services, I decided church was no longer for me. Simply put, the messages I received from my pastor were stern, fear-based, and limited to one perspective a seeming contrast to the information I received from the mountains, the trees and the Indian in the clouds.

In my conversations with the etheric world, I learned that there are many perspectives and that no one point of view is greater or less than another. I was confused by the idea that my religion would have me subscribe to the concept that the only way to heaven is to follow one man's path. Furthermore, I felt that heaven was Earth and that I was already home should I choose to perceive it that way. I had to wonder, "How could there be so many beliefs but only one correct answer?"

It was obvious to me that I could not be limited to one way of being when there were many roads to happiness. In that moment, my claircognizance knew the truth: there is never one answer, and all people have the right to what works best for them. Not begrudging my religion's assertions, as I still had reverence for the people in the Bible, I stopped attending church in an effort to discover my personal philosophies.

I've since researched many other world religions beyond Christianity, such as Islam, Judaism, and Buddhism, in an effort to gauge their perspectives against my own. What I found amazing about the world's major belief systems is that at their core, they all advocate the same ideals of love, peace and unity. Yet organized religions, worldwide and of all kinds, have been the primary instigators of horrific atrocities and wars. This contradiction in belief versus action doesn't make sense.

The problem is that most religions espouse that there is only one way to ascend into grace, denying the legitimacy of other beliefs. This denial to see the higher, quantum energetic understanding that there are many paths to enlightenment creates narrow perspectives, which in turn initiates dogma and the need to make people obey, yet again, for the sake of validating one's unconscious ego.

However, religious dogma seems to be on the decline in our transforming times. Pope Francis of the Catholic Church most notably demonstrated this shift away from hard-line beliefs toward more inclusive ideals when he stated that Christians owe gays and others an apology.

Interestingly, I also recently watched a video featuring a "Flash Meditation." Rather than a mob of people suddenly breaking into dance in a shopping mall, this group of around thirty individuals simultaneously sat down in the middle of a bustling crowd and began meditating. What I found most beautiful about this performance art was its nonviolent message of peace in oneself and peace in the world, which is exactly why they were using meditation as their symbol for achieving collective harmony. Inner reflection allows one to find higher understanding and acceptance for one's self and others.

You don't have to push against the ideals of another to assert your own, nor do you have to attend Sunday services. We are all uniquely different, and that makes us equals and deserving of contentment. One of the biggest keys to mending the world is to use your intuition to take back your right to discover your own truth. When you stop looking to outside sources to tell you what to believe and how to act and start following your inner promptings, then love, acceptance and cooperation become your self-realized commandments exuding serenity to all of humankind.

Now that you have had the opportunity to use your intuition to pay attention to the state of your foundational being, and you understand what you need in order to thrive in your personal circumstances, you can apply these same concepts to your relationships and life issues. Intentionally practice bringing your spirit into your everyday life so that you can live more of your ideal reality while also contributing to the betterment of all.

PART V

INTUITIVELY UNITED

Be Authentic and Bring Transparency to the World

"We have to dare to be ourselves, however frightening or strange that self may prove to be."

– Mary Sarton, Poet

CYNTHIA AND ANDREW had been married thirty five years. Cynthia described it as heaven. She was married to a man who had helped raise the children, loved to travel, supported her entrepreneurial spirit, and didn't expect her to follow traditional roles. Unfortunately, Andrew had a secret. It seems that Andrew was transgendered. Not wanting to hide his true nature any longer, Andrew told Cynthia he wanted to become a woman.

Cynthia was shocked. Although it had been over a decade since they had been intimate, Cynthia thought that was how all long-term couples co-existed. Learning that her husband didn't desire her left Cynthia feeling wounded and betrayed. "His lifetime of dishonesty has taken my best years and I will never have true love in my life now," Cynthia tearfully confided.

My heart went out to Cynthia. I've been rejected in love and understand the pain. I can't image how I'd feel if I'd spent thirty-five years with someone without knowing their deepest inner thoughts. However, in Andrew's defense, our culture has notoriously shunned gays, lesbians and the transgendered, not to mention differences of any kind. Only recently have our cultural views regarding sexual orientation started expanding and becoming more inclusive. You have to commend Andrew for stepping up and living his truth during a time when it is essential that every person do so, no matter their issue or cause, no matter the social perception.

Still, Cynthia was heartbroken. She wanted to know why this change in circumstances was happening to her. I knew that in order to help Cynthia find her heart's healing, it would be necessary to help her gain a much broader perspective of her personal soul's history and the karma that had drawn her and Andrew together, concepts she knew little about.

Have you ever thought of yourself as a soul? What if this wasn't the first time your spirit had inhabited a body? Throughout history, there have been many well-documented accounts of individuals recalling past lives. Most recently, the book *Soul Survivor: The Reincarnation of a World War II Fighter Pilot*, describes the modern-day tale of a young boy with vivid recollection of his previous lifetime.

When James Leininger was just two – and throughout his childhood in the early 2000's – he told his parents that he had been a World War II fighter pilot in his past life. James had frequent nightmares of being a man flying a plane and hearing gunfire all around him before crashing into the ocean and dying. So vivid was his past memory that James was even able to recall incredibly specific details about his previous life, like his jet's exact instrumentation, that he had been based on a ship named Natoma, that his name was James then also, and that he had been shot down over Iwo Jima.

With this information, James' parents researched military records and found that their son's description matched that of the life of James Huston, Jr., an American pilot stationed on the USS Natoma Bay, who had been killed in action in March 1945. James would eventually meet with some of the men from his former company who had survived the war, as well as some of Huston's remaining family members. During these visits, young James remembered facts and circumstances from the past that the boy should never have known.

James was fortunate. His parents could have told him to ignore the messages. They could have chastised him for having a vivid imagination. They even could have medicated him as if he had a mental disorder. Instead, they listened to their son and gave him room to express things they couldn't understand. In the end, recognizing James' past life not only allowed his soul to find peace but also brought healing to a war-torn generation, lessening the sadness of their losses with the certainty that there is life after death.

Cynthia would need to see herself from the expanded perspective of her soul in order to find her healing. When you see yourself from a more eternal perspective, your innate behaviors start to make more sense, giving you greater control over your actions, your reactions, and ultimately your experiences.

The problem is that our culture does not view individuals as energetic beings who can transfer their consciousness from body to body, which is unfortunate, as it limits what a person can experience. However, the laws of universal physics state that we are energetic beings, and energy never ceases to exist. Therefore, our soul's consciousness, being energetic, is eternal and can manifest itself into another body when it deems that it's necessary for growth. In fact, many ancient societies and religions place great importance on this concept of spiritual rebirth, believing that once a body dies, its soul will transfer into another physical vessel and continue its divine purpose.

Buddhists even evolved the Tibetan tradition of recognizing the reincarnated souls of particular scholar-adepts who had been immensely helpful in bringing knowledge and peace to all sentient beings. The Dalai Lama is one of these adepts. He is the fourteenth Dalai Lama, because that is the number of times the Tibetan Master has consciously manifested himself into another body in an effort to continue his work of inspiring enlightenment in the world.[xiii]

Cynthia had always been curious about the idea that she could have occupied a different form in another lifetime but had never considered whether or not it was true, let alone what impact her past could have on her in present time. Yet in order for Cynthia to discover her heart's healing, she would need to understand her soul's history and its subsequent karmic connection to Andrew.

While it is by the process of reincarnation that a soul moves through its experiences, karma ultimately determines what a soul will design for itself in order to continue its evolution. If you are like most people, you likely believe that karma is a force outside yourself that imposes judgment upon you for your deeds. However, karma is self-imposed. In that sense, there is no higher being judging your progress, there is only your belief about yourself and how you perceive your experiences. For instance, if your soul judges itself worthy of its expressions, it generates energetic lightness in your being. When you judge yourself as unworthy, you amass a darkness or heaviness in your soul. Either way, you have created karma for yourself. That magnetic force will then cause your soul to generate circumstances that either reinforce your positive beliefs or tear down your negative ideals so that you can continue to expand your awareness.

When I witness a person's karmic relationships, I use the intuitive symbol of a mirror. The reflections I witness tell me a great deal about a couple, both past and present, together and individually. As I looked into a mirror reflecting both Cynthia and Andrew, I first noticed several men standing behind Andrew. These men represented his past lives. Upon further examination, I could see that the group seemed similar in character with their stuffy appearances, surly attitudes, and oppressive feel.

Instantly, I sensed that Andrew's soul had lived several lifetimes as a man who had been severely unkind to women, children and the environment. Although in his previous incarnations he was simply going along with the cycle of time, these past lives were weighing heavily on Andrew's soul. His spirit didn't agree with being brutal and mean. As a result, Andrew developed a self-judgment regarding his masculinity. That karmic view then prompted Andrew's soul to design a lifetime in which he could break free of his outdated male character and live more of his true compassionate and loving nature.

Cynthia commented on how Andrew had always rejected his father's ideals. Andrew's dad was former military, as was his grandfather and great-grandfather before him. As the only boy, Andrew's father expected him to follow the same service-driven path. However, Andrew worked hard and earned a full scholarship to become an engineer, ending the family tradition. It seemed clear to me that Andrew's soul had created his early masculine rebellion so that he could one day accomplish his greater goal of transitioning into his feminine essence.

With this insight into Andrew's soul history, Cynthia felt empathy for her husband and his motivations. In that moment, her heart softened with relief and deeper love. However, to find complete healing, Cynthia still needed to know what karmic judgments she held about herself that had caused her soul to create a partnership with Andrew.

Clairvoyantly, I looked into the mirror, this time seeking Cynthia's karma. My first impression was that of Cynthia wearing layers of clothing from multiple eras of time and feeling oppressed and overly burdened. Observing the scene further, I witnessed Cynthia's feminine essence emerge from under the pile of clothes, as if it had disassociated from its expressions and was no longer inhabiting her body. I asked why Cynthia's female nature did not want to experience its circumstances.

I learned that Cynthia's feminine essence had fragmented due to multiple lifetimes of having to endure roles, behaviors and circumstances chosen for her by a cruel world. Consequently, her feminine nature had stopped engaging and was no longer evolving.

Your soul has inhabited both male and female lifetimes. However, undeniably, the past five thousand years of history has been unjust toward women of all races and beliefs. Most souls choosing a feminine embodiment during man's dark history have endured abuse, persecution and death simply for being a woman. Thankfully, that period has ended. Consequently, we all can achieve balance now, which is why so many souls have chosen to incarnate at this time. Today, souls have the opportunity to reconcile their karmic past, thereby healing themselves and creating a brighter future.

Cynthia's soul certainly needed reconciliation, as it was no longer willing to be present and was therefore not growing in expression. Consequently, in this lifetime, her soul had designed circumstances that would allow her to transform her karmic beliefs about men and relationships. By creating a connection with a non-traditional man who would not treat her like a possession but would allow her spirit to soar, Cynthia's spirit could finally feel safe inhabiting her body again, shifting her karmic patterns and healing her soul. What better partner to help Cynthia fulfill her needs than Andrew?

Cynthia divulged that she had never really enjoyed intimacy and was thankful that her husband wasn't more amorous. At the same time, she loved his companionship and that his income supported them, as it afforded her the luxury of a sustainable life and the opportunity to explore her desires.

Upon realizing that their souls were perfectly suited to one another, Cynthia once again felt contentment in her marriage. In the end, Cynthia and Andrew (now Sarah) remained married. Cynthia understood that Sarah's soul needed to live her truth, which Cynthia fully supported. In return, Cynthia would experience a gentle and kind partnership built on equality, restoring her own feminine empowerment and love for the masculine.

In this section, you will use your intuition to heal your soul's karmic patterns personally and with family and to heal your sense of purpose and your ability to maintain an intimate partnership. As you apply your higher knowledge in your everyday relationships, you become a thought leader, reinventing yourself and your family values, thinking globally and loving universally, all while anchoring a healthier standard for living with the power to transform the American ideal.

Heal Karmic Patters and Create Equality

"How we live this life determines what we are in the next."

– Paramahansa Yogananda, Spiritual Leader

VERONICA HAD BEEN my friend for many years. She was an intelligent and driven woman who was finishing her master's degree when she suddenly started experiencing excessive anxiety and heart palpitations. In fact, the attacks were so acute that they were keeping her from completing her studies. Veronica had been to several doctors and had undergone many tests, but nothing had come back abnormal. Unfortunately, her severe distress persisted with no explanation or cure in sight. She turned to me, hoping I could see something to help the doctors find the answer to her physical ailment.

Setting my intentions to witness the symbolism in Veronica's field that represented her illness, I saw a large pocket of stagnant energy sitting in her chest that felt ancient, as if it had been there for eons of time. Realizing that the unmoving mass was responsible for Veronica's pain, I asked to see the source of the stagnation, looking for clues on how to restore it to a healthy state of flow.

As the mass drew me in, a landscape started to unfold. I could see a lush jungle all around, vibrating with the cacophony of tropical birds, animals and various insects. Even the humidity was palpable. Viewing the scene further, I noticed an enormous Mayan temple in front of me. Moving closer to the structure, I realized that a ceremony of sorts was taking place. However, this was a celebration I would rather have not seen.

Hundreds of people had gathered at the foot of the pyramid steps. A large stone altar rested on a platform several feet up the temple. There I could see a Mayan priest preparing the sacred space for the event, laying out various tools such as bone-handled knives, ornate gold cups and a feathered smudge stick.

I then watched as two large men escorted Veronica, who resembled a Mayan woman, to the altar, tightly holding on to her as if they were concerned she might try to run. It was then I realized that the celebration was really a ritual sacrifice honoring the Gods, and Veronica was the main attraction.

Suddenly, I felt all of Veronica's anxiety well up, with her chest wanting to explode. Asking how she'd come to be in this predicament, I was given the sense that Veronica's Mayan father had offered his daughter to the priest in hopes that it would elevate his status in the community. Unfortunately, Veronica had no say in the matter. As the dagger pierced through her heart, against her will, Veronica was sacrificed that day.

Interestingly, as I was relaying the scene to Veronica, she suddenly began feeling anxious, lightheaded and in need of fresh air. As I followed her outdoors, she said to me, "Do you think this is why I passed out in high school during a film about the Mayans?"

Apparently, when Veronica attended high school, her class was learning about the Mayan culture. She said that they had been watching a film about the indigenous people's lifestyle when she had a sudden panic attack and passed out during the presentation. She said that something about the film had made her uneasy. She had begun feeling nauseous and couldn't control her body's responses. Since that time, she had not had another such episode. Then again, she was in the habit of staying away from all things Mayan.

It would seem that Veronica's native lifetime was having a profound impact on her current reality. Curious as to why she was once again experiencing difficulty with this past lifetime, I asked Veronica what was happening in present time that might mirror her past. Instantly, she understood where her prior circumstances were patterning today.

It would seem that Veronica's father in present time wanted her to work for him at the family business after finishing school. However, Veronica had other ideas. She wanted to establish a career that would allow her to travel the world, contributing to ideals that would make Earth a better place. The only problem was that her father was an insistent man, and she was having a hard time saying no to his request.

It was then that I realized that Veronica was used to being the sacrificial lamb, fulfilling the needs of others before her own. Veronica's father in this life may not have been her father from the past, but it was clear that she was resonating with a sense that she had no control over the situation. However, there was one big difference between her earlier life and now, suggesting that she was the only one in command of her reality.

Veronica's present day father was offering his daughter empowerment, not sacrifice. He had fostered her knowledge, providing her with an excellent education. Her father also valued her strengths and trusted her abilities to make sound business decisions. In every way, Veronica's father today was giving her what she needed to live an empowered future in any way her spirit needed, whether with him or out in the world.

In the end, Veronica followed her personal path. As her pain ceased, she graduated with honors and procured a position with a global company mediating worldwide change, which her father proudly supports, cheering her on every step of the way.

As you have seen in other stories, physical illness doesn't always have a present-time cause. Veronica's unhappy emotions at being the sacrifice sparked a memory in her body that required an emotional and spiritual response. Emotionally she needed to speak her truth, and spiritually she needed to follow her unique path, as this was her road to healing and expansion.

Are you drawn to certain places or people? Do you have irrational fears that don't make sense in the context of your life today? Let's explore your soul's history so that you can become aware of the influences your many lifetimes have on you now.

Remember Your Soul's History

Witnessing your past lives is one of the best ways to discover the nature of your patterns. For instance, I once hosted a gathering where I witnessed the past lives of the guests, helping them discover the meaning and healing in their lives. One of the previous lifetimes I saw was for a young woman who in her past had been the mother of five children with another on the way, raising them in oppressive conditions and struggling just to feed them. Honestly, she looked miserably unhappy and wished she could escape her fate.

When I asked the woman where she thought this past life was showing up for her today, she was shocked. Apparently, the young lady had been seriously contemplating whether she wanted to be a mother or not. In many ways, she found pregnancy to be repulsive and was leaning toward not having children but didn't know why she felt that way.

Armed with the knowledge of her previous lifetime, the young woman was able to understand what was driving her impulses. More importantly, she could now consciously determine what she would prefer today. Perhaps she could now reconsider motherhood knowing she could stop after one or two children. Or perhaps she could now choose not to have children knowing that she was opting for a lifetime of self discovery and exploration. Either way, she was now aware of how the past was influencing her and could make an informed choice about her future. The intuitive exercise below will guide you toward finding a past life and discerning its affect on your current circumstances.

1. To begin, follow the Standard Preparation for All Intuitive Explorations found in the back.

2. Next, find your past life by using your cornerstone instincts to reveal a landscape on your viewing screen. Observe the scenery, taking in the setting and surroundings. Notice the weather and time of day. Also get a sense of what region of the world in which this place exists.

3. Now get a sense of the era in which you find yourself by looking at the fashion of the time. Look for people, observing how they go about their days, giving yourself a general idea of where you are and what is taking place around you.

4. Next, ask to see yourself. Notice if you are masculine or feminine in this lifetime. Look at how you are dressed and determine what that might tell you about yourself and your role in this life.

5. Simply watch as your past life unfolds, noticing how you move about your days and the purpose you enact. Take note of the state of your health, family, and relationships. Determine how you feel about your circumstances.

6. Also notice if anyone in your present life, such as your mother, sister, or neighbor was with you in some capacity in the past. Who were they and what was their impact on you?

7. Once you have taken plenty of time to watch your story unfold, notice your death scene. Observe who was with you, what your cause of death was, how you felt about it and what was taking place at the time.

8. Allow yourself to gain an understanding of who you were in this past life, the affect it had upon your experiences then, and how it might be affecting you in present time.

When you have completed your past-life assessment, ask yourself the following questions to get a better sense of how this life influences you today and how you can grow from it:

- What was the landscape of my past life? Was it day, night, winter, or summer? How did I feel about the setting?

- In what region of the world was this past life? What was the era?

- What was taking place in my scene? Did I notice people? What were they doing?

- Where was I in the landscape? Was I male or female, young or old?

- What was my role in my past life? How did I feel about my life emotionally, mentally, physically and spiritually?

- What was the state of my health, family, and relationships?

- Was there anyone from my present life with me in the past? Who were they? What was their role then versus now?

- What caused my death? Was anyone with me, or was I alone? How did I feel about my life and what happened to my spirit when it left my body?

- What was I learning in my past lifetime?

- What patterns do I enact today as a result of my past life? Are those behaviors beneficial or not?

- Are there any patterns I would like to change as a result of witnessing my past life? How will those changes make my life better?

- How does witnessing my past lives help me in my everyday circumstances?

Let Your Past Life Assist You Today

I've seen many past lives for myself, all of which have a profound impact on me now. However, the reason it's important to understand your past lives is to learn the nature of your personal patterns. Contrary to traditional psychology, your mother isn't the source of all your life issues.

Your soul is unique, forming itself from a compilation of all its expressions. In that sense, when you are born, you bring your eternal essence with you. Your fundamental nature then becomes the filter by which you process your life experiences and ultimately dictates how you will react to your environment. This is why twins growing up with the exact same environmental influences can have differing ideals and opinions about their experiences and life in general.

Part of being a co-creator of reality means being responsible for the patterns of behavior you brought with you into this life that may be creating discord in some capacity. When you see the pattern from a past perspective, you instantly understand where that life's blueprint is playing out in your current reality, giving you the opportunity to change your circumstances into something that better suits your character today.

Use your past life discoveries to aid you in healing your present-time behaviors. Below is a suggestion for how to work with the information you received in your past life exploration so that you can achieve greater personal and collective balance.

Patterns take time to change. You generally have to work on shifting an ideal for several months before it will ingrain into something new, like training a vine where to climb. I find it best to revisit the lifetime through several active meditations. Take time with this process, focusing on learning the past lesson and instituting new ways of being in the present.

Evolve Your Thinking

Of course, it will be necessary to uncover the thoughts you have about the idea of living past lives, specifically listening for negative thoughts such as, "I'm making all this up," "The past cannot affect me today," or "The past was better than the present." You will want to shift any limiting thought you have to something more positive.

"My intuition shows me the things I need to see for a good reason."

"It's easy to see where my past life patterns show up today."

"I don't want to relive my experiences. I want to expand upon them."

Intuition's Ability to Reconcile Your Relationships

Many years ago when I interviewed guests on my talk radio show, one person particularly had a visceral impact on me. Ted was a "trained psychologist and self-taught metaphysician," he joked. However, it was my interactions with Ted that changed my views of others and myself forever. No longer would I see differences in people. Instead, I could find common ground and equality with everyone regardless of their gender, race or orientation, thereby instituting peace in the world.

I met Ted at a talk we were both attending regarding extrasensory perception. A friend of mine was enthralled with Ted, as he had one of those larger-than-life reputations that everyone admired. However, I found him to be a bit of a know-it-all, and I wasn't particularly keen on his character for reasons I couldn't really explain. There was something about Ted that I instantly didn't like despite the community's high praise of him.

Pushing my feelings aside, I invited Ted to be a guest on the show to discuss energy and the unseen world, to which he excitedly agreed. However, in the time it took to coordinate schedules, I became feverish and nauseous and had to immediately excuse myself so that I could go into the restroom and vomit. I left the event assuming I had come down with the flu. The next morning, however, I felt fine. Expecting to be chilled and aching, I was grateful to feel energetic and ready to start a new day.

Several weeks later, I called Ted to confirm our interview, and immediately after he picked up the phone, my mysterious sickness resurfaced. Again, I was feverish and needing to throw up. Making the conversation quick, I found it odd that my interactions with Ted were making me ill, but I was too exhausted to do anything about it. Instead, I slept off the infection, later awaking to my restored health.

When the morning of my interview with Ted arrived, I began getting sick once again. Finally reaching my limit with the issue, I decided to take matters into my own hands. Using my intuition, I would witness the energy between Ted and me to see if I could discover the source of my mysterious illness. Little did I know that my actions to uncover the truth would result in my heightened acceptance and love for all people.

Using my intuition, I witnessed the past-life karma between Ted and me. At first, I noticed his spirit standing in front of me. Curiously, I saw an energetic cord connecting us from stomach to stomach and knew that this exchange was causing my sickness. Cords represent our agreements with others and how we are all working together to evolve our souls. Energetic cords can also carry within them the karma between individuals that might be pertinent to their growth, as was the case with me and Ted.

Needing to understand our energetic draw in order to heal myself, I focused my intuition on the cord. Feeling as if I'd been pulled into a wormhole, my consciousness was suddenly whisked back in time to fifteenth century England. I could see a woman, who I instantly recognized as me, standing in a flat above a bustling city mercantile. The studio seemed to be a laboratory of sorts, as it had tables lined with beakers, test tubes, and several varieties of elixirs brewing.

Observing the past scene further, I then saw a man resembling Ted occupying the flat as well, mixing drinks to toast our accomplishments. I got the distinct impression that we were alchemists who had concocted a prize-winning tincture that we were going to present to the king and queen. Unfortunately, upon drinking Ted's celebratory treat, I witnessed myself getting violently sick, as if I'd been poisoned. As I fell to the floor gasping for air, Ted coldly and calculatingly gathered the book containing our volumes of work, claiming them as his own and leaving me for dead.

Shocked by the scene, I didn't know what to think. I certainly didn't think Ted intended to harm me today. Yet I also couldn't ignore the physical ramifications that the past was still having on my physical being. Seeking

155

guidance, I asked the universe to help me understand what I could do to end this unnecessary karma.

Suddenly my consciousness shifted to another scene. This time I was in an empty courtroom. My first thought was that perhaps Ted hadn't gotten away with my murder and I was about to watch his trial. Except there was no judge and Ted never arrived. Observing the scene further, I realized that the light coming through the windows and the design of the space conveyed that this was another place and time.

Looking around the courtroom, I noticed an old man, an English barrister, seated at a large table with several manuscripts of various sizes and subjects strewn about its top. Focusing my attention on the lawyer, I was suddenly aware that he was me, or rather I was him. It seemed that I was seeing my spirit's next incarnation after being poisoned.

As I stood in wonder, I watched as I, the barrister, opened a large book containing complex alchemical cures. Immediately, I recognized the author's name. It was Ted, and this was our work that he had published as his own a hundred years earlier. When the barrister saw the name on the book, an irrational emotion of fear and dread consumed him, and he slammed the text shut, deeming it heretical and banning it from public consumption.

In that moment, two things went through my mind. First, I had banned books for being heretical? I would never have thought I could do such a thing, except I completely understood the barrister's unconscious motives. Second, I had to wonder how long Ted and I had been stuck in a loop of judging each other, creating our karmic pattern of 'you do me wrong, I do you wrong.'

Regardless of how long the pattern had existed, it needed to end. At this point in my intuitive exploration, I asked Ted's spirit to join me in present time. As I saw Ted standing before me again in my inner forum, I expressed forgiveness for myself and him. I understood that in our pasts, we had been individuals living from our egoic lower minds and operating under unconscious circumstances. I then expressed to Ted's spirit that I was going to cut the cord between us, freeing myself from the dynamic and that he could do whatever he needed to with his portion of the energy.

After finishing my intuitive energy work, I reset myself by grounding, claiming my space and setting healthy boundaries. Gratefully, I felt well again. My sickness was gone, and I was certain that I could interact with Ted without any further negative ramifications. Interestingly, two hours later I received an unexpected call from Ted telling me that he would not be able to make our interview, because he had suddenly become ill with the flu. Without a doubt, I felt that I had reconciled my karma with Ted.

What do you think might happen if the world's governments, particularly in the Middle East, looked at their past-life karma? They would likely find that their souls have been both Palestinian and Israeli, devout and agnostic, and black and white at some time in their history. Imagine how different that might make them feel toward themselves and one another.

Karma is the great equalizer. When you see your totality, you understand that you have been both the victim and the aggressor. Having to find peace within yourself between your lightness and darkness suddenly heightens your perspective, giving you access to greater forgiveness, acceptance and compassion for yourself and others.

One of the perspectives you would benefit from adopting today is to recognize that your soul has been masculine, feminine, black, red, white, pagan, Christian, disabled and whole (to name a few). You have also likely experienced wealth, poverty, power, support, weakness, and isolation. In other words, you've run the gamut of life experiences. When you can accept the truth of yourself and others, good, bad and indifferent, you can then recognize equality among the genders and people of all nationalities, races and religions.

Discover Your Family Role and Heal Your Soul Group

"The way you help heal the world is to start with your own family."

– Mother Teresa, Saint

IT WOULD SEEM that every family has its wayward member, and for Kimberly it was her sister. Unlike the rest of the family, Kimberly refused to give up on her sister, despite her blatant manipulations, emotional neediness, toxic relationships, and lack of consideration for others. The problem was that Kimberly's noble need to care take of her sister was causing a strain on Kimberly's marriage. The sister demanded a lot of Kimberly's time, which meant that Kimberly often left her husband and children to fend for themselves, creating emotional issues at home.

Kimberly sought out my intuitive services, because her husband had given her an ultimatum. It was either the sister or him. Yet Kimberly believed that you never discard family, although she wasn't sure how to hone her husband's needs while also serving those of her sister.

I suggested to Kimberly that we intuitively witness her family karma and the role her soul was agreeing to play in order to aid in the group's evolution.

This higher understanding would help Kimberly determine her healthiest stance with all the members of her clan, not just her husband and sister.

Interestingly, there are many layers of development for souls to embody. As a result, there are new, young, mature and old souls growing on earth. A new soul might be having an experience in a third-world country, learning the basics of survival. A young soul may be living as an oil tycoon, imposing his self-indulgent power over others for the sake of mastering his ego. The mature soul could be your neighbor, trying alternative medicines for the first time. And an old soul may be a healer, imparting wisdom to those in need.

Souls that are developing at the same pace generally combine in their evolutionary goals, creating families. These families consist of several souls, each playing a specific role such as father, aunt, sister or grandmother. These souls will commune with one another prior to physical incarnation to decide which familial representation is best for each of their individual growths, as well as the expansion of the whole. The souls then embody themselves in their family group agreements. Over many lifetimes, these soul groups will embody a reality, changing positions with each new plan. In other words, you might be a mother to a daughter today, but in the past, the two of you could have been brothers.

Ultimately, the souls will determine if a positive or negative expression is necessary in order to fulfill the group ideals. Sometimes a soul-group plan requires that a member assume a negative stance, like being insensitive or even abusive, in order to prompt the group's growth, which can seem harsh. However, intuition tells us that these negative spins are necessary when full consciousness does not exist between all parties.

For example, if a woman's husband abandoned the family, leaving her to raise the kids alone, his negative stance could be seen as a higher agreement. Perhaps the mother's soul is learning independence while also teaching the children the values of being part of family. This type of negative agreement could be a way of evolving the next generation through love and higher understanding.

Remember, you are only now recognizing your karmic pasts and the deeper wounding and life patterns you must heal. Because you have not been trained like the Dalai Lama to obtain recall of your past knowledge, it can be necessary at times to re-experience a negative pattern in order to understand what needs to change. It was important that Kimberly be aware of this tough love concept within soul groups. Having a full-scope perspective and the ability to see all sides of the situation would allow Kimberly to discover what her sister truly needed in order to achieve her higher goals.

When I intuitively witness a soul group's dynamic, I use the symbolism of the tree. To me, trees represent family and familial beliefs. When I clairvoyantly witness a tree for a soul group, what I observe will tell me a lot about how the unit is functioning. I might see a 300-year-old oak with abundant leaves, nuts and birds, telling me that the group is healthy, thriving and likely very supportive of one another. If I see a newly planted maple sapling with a healthy trunk, three sturdy branches coming into bloom, and roots that are digging in and forging their stability, it tells me that this is a small family unit, perhaps a single mom successfully raising young kids on her own with little support but herself.

When I witnessed a tree for Kimberly's family, I didn't see just one tree. I saw an entire community of tall, thin Italian cypress trees working together to harvest grapes for wine. Chuckling at the picture, I continued to observe. It was a beautiful scene set in a wide sprawling Tuscan villa with several acres of grape vines hanging from trellised lines. I was impressed with how well the winery was operating. Each cypress had a responsibility and seemed to be busily doing its part.

However, upon closer inspection, I noticed two trees in the group that were not fulfilling their duties. One was reclining in the sun, and the other one was hiding out altogether, avoiding its chores while nibbling on the harvest. Being the intuitive detective, I asked the image if Kimberly and her sister were the two deadbeat trees. Immediately, my attention shifted to another cypress that was frantically completing her tasks while also trying to finish the chores of the trees not pulling their weight. Instantly, I knew that Kimberly was the overworked cypress and that her harried pace could not continue.

As I relayed the scene to Kimberly, she interjected an unexpected giggle and said, "My husband and I own a family-run microbrewery." I laughed and shook my head at the scene of the winery I'd just witnessed. Symbolism and intuition never cease to amaze me in the way that they convey and receive messages accurately without having to be exact.

Kimberly then informed me that her sister worked at the business, although she would rarely show up unless it was payday. Furthermore, Kimberly's sister wasn't the only wayward member of the family not doing her part. There was a cousin mimicking the sister in many ways.

It would seem that Kimberly's soul group had two members who were not growing. Asking to find clarity regarding why these souls were shirking their responsibilities, my attention quickly diverted to the image of a majestic diamond necklace that felt as if countless generations of aristocracy had inherited its beauty. Watching the scene unfold, I witnessed a wealthy and powerful man fasten the necklace on a woman, whom I perceived was Kimberly's sister in a past life.

It was 18th century France. Kimberly's sister came from a family of lesser means. However, when the sister fortuitously met the affluent heir, suddenly she saw a way to escape her life of hard work and poverty. The sister quickly set her motives toward trapping the young gentleman, and it worked. Unfortunately, the aristocrat's mother had other ideas for her son and poisoned Kimberly's sister before she could give birth.

Interestingly, my recounting seemed to validate for Kimberly something she had always sensed about her sister. Apparently, the sister had elaborate tastes and fanciful ideas of marrying into wealth. Kimberly also shared that her husband felt that he was not just supporting Kimberly but her sister as well. He was growing resentful of the situation and wanted it to end. Kimberly's husband didn't think her sister should work at the family business anymore, believing she wouldn't grow up until she could take care of her own needs.

Given the karmic past I'd seen for Kimberly's sister, I agreed with her husband. The sister's karma in believing that money and prominence would make life easy had proven false. Her task in this life was to rise to her challenges and put in the effort necessary to fulfill herself. I then suggested that we witness Kimberly's karma in order to examine the role she was agreeing to play in her sister's evolution to see if she was meeting her part of the soul-group bargain.

My first impression of Kimberly was of pure light. She was the sun that was warming, enlivening and encouraging the trees in her family. Immediately, I knew that she was an old soul and that her karmic contract with her family was to provide them with encouragement and light so that they could fulfill the needs of their souls. The only problem was that the sister was overly reliant on Kimberly to do things for her that she was unwilling to do for herself.

In order for Kimberly to fulfill her familial contracts properly, she would need to apply a negative spin or tough love to her normally sweet nature and firmly say no to her sister's unreasonable demands. Once she applied this element of strength and proper use of power, she could then reassume her enlightened stance, encouraging her sister to grow into her greatest expressions.

Months later Kimberly checked in with me. She said it wasn't easy to change her ideals about family and the need to rescue her sister, but something about the message from our previous session had felt correct. Kimberly confided that she didn't know if being tough with her sister was the right thing to do, but she knew she had to do something different. Interestingly, after firing the sister from the family business, the sister found a position as a receptionist, where she was learning to be timely, accountable and financially responsibly. Kimberly thought her sister was gaining tremendous confidence in herself.

However, what was most rewarding was hearing Kimberly's relief at no longer being responsible for her sister's needs. Instead, Kimberly was giving her time and attention to her husband, her children and those in her family willing to be personally responsible. As a result, Kimberly was creating deeper bonds and loyalties among her immediate soul group, which enriched her with greater love, contentment and joy.

One of the biggest problems we have with the family dynamic today is that we are unaware of the higher perspective and purpose of our soul groups. As admirable as your ideas and thoughts are about family, never wanting any member to suffer, you cannot save them from the experiences needed to achieve their soul's growth. At the same time, you cannot depend on family to do things for you that you are unwilling to do for yourself lest you stop your own soul's evolution. This is where your intuition becomes critical in striking the balance between family support and individual responsibility. Let's explore your soul's karma and the role you play in the evolution of your family.

Redefine Your Family Role

Just as you have personal karma, your soul-group has ingrained patterns from past beliefs that need evolving as well. Family karmic energy resides in your field as a genetic predisposition toward certain patterns like alcoholism, heart failure, and balding. When a soul group experiences these types of generational, repeating issues, it's a sign that the group needs some form of evolution. Perhaps they must learn emotional stability, love for one's self, or even how to shed vanity. At some point, one of the soul group members, or perhaps several, will devise lifetimes for themselves with the task of healing the genetic issue, not just for themselves but for the entire group. Whether that means overcoming alcoholism, stabilizing the heart through positive self-reinforcement or by becoming comfortable with all aspects of one's appearance, once the issue is resolved, the entire soul group, including its generations to come, is freed of the karma. Below is an intuitive exercise exploring your karmic-family role and the larger purpose you play in transforming the whole.

1. Start by following the Standard Preparation for All Intuitive Explorations in the reference section.
2. When you have completed the customary steps, begin your exploration by imagining your family and contemplating your soul

group's genetic patterns, such as what issues persist from generation to generation that need transforming into higher expressions.

3. When you have considered your family's karma, ask to see a tree that represents your family dynamics in present time.

4. Take a minute to observe your tree fully. Notice the type of tree it is, its size, color and foliage. Look at the branches and leaves. Does it have fruit, nuts, pinecones or flowers? Also, get a sense of the tree's overall appearance and health.

5. Determine what part of the tree you represent in this lifetime. Are you a part of the roots, branches, fruit, soil, water or sunlight? Find the role you play in the forming of this tree.

6. Once you understand your function within the group, determine the functions of your mom, dad, aunt, brother, children, cousin, etc. and what part of the tree they are responsible for maintaining.

7. Finally, ask to see a role you've played in another lifetime that might be influencing you and your family dynamic today.

When you have completed your assessment of your soul group's family tree and each member's agreement, ask yourself the following questions:

• What type of tree represented my family? What does this tell me about myself and my soul group?

• What was the specific condition of my family tree? What might this say about my soul group as a unit?

• What part of the tree represented me and my functions within the soul group today?

• Am I fulfilling my soul's contracts within my family? What implication does this have in my life and my family's lives?

• Are the other members of my soul group fulfilling their family agreements? What implications are their actions having on the family unit?

• What individual roles have I played with my family in the past? What was the result?

- What can I do personally to enact a healthier family dynamic for myself and the group?
- How does witnessing my family from a higher perspective help me and them in our everyday lives?

Maintain a Healthy Family

Once you have examined your family structure and karma, you can assume responsibility for your portion of the soul group's growth. This will require that you be exceptionally honest with yourself and the group about establishing new beliefs, behaviors and standards that support your higher understandings. Below are a few suggestions to help you maintain your new healthy family dynamic:

1. Start each day by reaffirming your commitment to understanding and assuming responsibility to your higher family-karmic role. Remind yourself of how you are personally evolving and how that will benefit the whole.
2. Take positive actions with your family that support your new understanding. Recognize when you slip back into old patterns, and make a point to adapt to your higher function.
3. Establish traditions around your new ideals. For instance, many years ago I assumed the role of matriarch for our group. Upon doing so, I changed the way we operate at the holidays in an effort to make our special times more about connection and less about material items. If you are like Kimberly, taking the role of cheerleader, you could enact a tradition in which once a month the family gets together or has a texting day in which everyone shares their most recent accomplishments. Or if you have a family that is dysfunctional to the degree that it is unhealthy for you to have relationships with them, create a new family through friends and partnership, and let that become your new tradition.

4. Your family dynamics and foundations have the biggest impact on your life. Regardless of your specific circumstances, get creative and find new expressions to support everyone's growth. Use your intuition to help remember your group's plan as well as your role within it so that you can establish the foundations that every member needs to thrive.

Evolve Your Thinking

The last thing to consider when balancing your group is to retrain any negative thoughts you have about family, transforming them into higher ideals that support everyone. Listen for the thoughts you have that are similar to these: "I hate my family," "My family doesn't understand me," or "My family can't function without me," and change those thoughts so that they are supportive of the entire group. Use the suggestions below, or have fun creating your own.

"I have the perfect family for what I'm here to learn and grow into."

"It's fine if my family doesn't understand me. I can know who I am."

"My family needs independence and a chance to figure the world out for themselves."

Intuition's Role in Creating Family Bonds

The landscape of the American family has changed dramatically in the past one hundred years. We've gone from treating our children as laborers, sending them to work in factories for eighteen hours six days a week to buying them everything their hearts demand even when they don't know the value of earning it for themselves. We've also gone from seeing men as the primary, if not only, bread winners in families to seeing more women than men enrolled in college and assuming the high-paying careers with dads staying at home to raise the kids. While it would seem that the picture of family is an ever-transitioning ideal, one element is unchanging regardless of the time. You can come from the richest or the poorest of families, but if you have a sense of belonging, you have wealth beyond compare.

Humanity has always shown a strong instinct to bond. We see that we are separate in physical form, yet we also have an internal knowingness that we are connected, initiating our desire to be one with others. Creating family units is our first step toward fulfilling our need to belong to something other than self. Interestingly however, many families devise a series of expectations that their group must meet in order to prove that they are worthy of acceptance, such as, "you must only love the opposite gender," or "do as you are told and not what you think." Unfortunately, these requirements often become our resistances, because our hearts seek unconditional acceptance yet receive guidelines for what is and is not loveable in a person based on arbitrary selection.

When my sister was younger and was showing signs of becoming an alcoholic, I would say to my family, "She just needs you to love her, even with her shortcomings, and then you can help her find a better way." My words fell on deaf ears, and instead, my sister was spurned and made to feel inferior for her seeming character flaw. It was then that my sister's inferiority complex drove her deeper into addiction and, eventually, mental illness. One has to wonder whether giving my sister's soul what it needed through unconditional love, regardless of the group's expectations, if that would have allowed her to create healthier circumstances. Perhaps armed with the sense of self-worth that accompanies belonging, my sister could have given up her negative patterns long before they became debilitating diseases. Unfortunately, we will never know now.

Discipline is always necessary, but when a person feels as though they are received, they learn to find their own way easier. Love and acceptance are critical elements in the development of an individual. When a soul desires to belong in family, it is seeking the value of unconditional receptivity. This sense of belonging allows a soul to establish sustainable foundations, supporting its growth over a lifetime.

Part of the trend toward higher living today requires that you use your intuition to rise above petty family gossip and unrealistic ideals of behavior, status and achievement, allowing unconditional love to bond you and your group. When children grow up under these inclusive ideals, they naturally become happy, peaceful and purposeful individuals, creating a balanced world.

Find Your Life's Plan and Transform the American Agenda

"The purpose of life is to live it, to taste experience to the utmost, to reach out eagerly and without fear for newer and richer experience."

— Eleanor Roosevelt, Former First Lady of the United States

FIONA HAD BEEN a graphic designer, nurse, salesperson, and most recently, a real-estate agent under the direction of her mother. When I met Fiona, she was ready to shift careers again and wondered if I could foretell her life's purpose. I looked at Fiona and said, "Pilot, you are supposed to be a pilot." She looked at me with bewilderment and replied, "I don't even like to fly."

Laughing at myself, I explained to Fiona that I couldn't read her fate, as that was still open to interpretation based on her point of awareness at any given time. What I could do, however, was help her discover her spirit's propensities so that she could consciously determine her own best purpose.

Just as I use trees to witness family dynamics, I use paths to symbolize a person's higher potentials and opportunities. Fiona's paths were plenty. There was a hot air balloon trail, a cobblestone walkway and even a passageway lined with baby strollers, just to name few. I could understand

171

why it was difficult for her to settle on one direction; the paths were just too inviting not to want to walk them all. Yet the more I observed the scene, the more one course seemed to shine brighter than the others.

The trail was a lush green grass path lined with flowers of all colors and warmed by sunlight. As I continued to walk the path, it seemed to meld into a turn-of-the-century New England settlement. The town's main street was comprised of a series of façade-front businesses, all similar in design and color – wooden structures with small windows and hanging signs to advertise their services. One storefront, however, was unlike all the others, and the path led directly to its front door.

The building resembled a house made of tall hedges, a flower-filled roof, and an arched wooden trellis ushering you into the establishment. I could even smell eucalyptus, frankincense and other medicinal essences as I entered, feeling as though I was walking into an ancient healing garden that Fiona's soul had once operated.

After I shared the scene with Fiona, she told me that nursing and healthcare were her true passions. Apparently, Fiona had earned a degree in nursing because she loved taking care of people. However, hospital politics caused her to focus more on coding the computer correctly and less on the needs of her patients. She said that the environment just didn't fit her, and she couldn't see herself going back.

I clarified for Fiona that her soul's potential as a healing professional might not be in a traditional setting; the garden of her past revealed alternative opportunities. Fiona could choose to be a holistic nutritionist, reiki master, or even a naturopathic doctor, bringing her healing nature to others in ways that better suited her nature. I encouraged Fiona to research her unconventional options, as this would likely fit her higher ideals.

However, it was also essential that Fiona recognize that her soul had many fulfilling purposes and that she didn't have to pick just one. If you recall, another path I'd seen available to Fiona was one of motherhood. When I said this, Fiona beamed with sheer delight. She wanted children more than she wanted anything but didn't think that could be a worthy pursuit. I assured Fiona that being a mother was just as important a role as being president of the United States.

I suggested Fiona think about how she could meld her passion for healing with her desire to raise a family. Designing a lifestyle that accommodated both Fiona's individual and collective yearnings would allow her soul to experience expanded fulfillment.

I saw Fiona a week later when she came to my intuitive development class. She hadn't decided which alternative field she wanted to immerse herself in, but whatever it was, she was going to bring her intuition into it so that she could always find her soul's unique path. You can explore your soul's many paths to purposeful fulfillment now.

Explore Your Purpose

You can make anything in life a purpose, such as being a mother, becoming a lawyer, starting your own business or feeding the hungry. However, purpose isn't about the titles you assume. If you are evolving yourself and contributing to the betterment of others, you are living a purposeful life and creating a harmonious world. As you explore your soul's unique potentials, know that your focuses continually change as you move through the phases of your life. In that sense, your ideas of what constitutes purpose are flexible and will shift over time. Follow the techniques below to discover your evolutionary leap into higher living.

1. Begin as usual by following the Standard Preparation for All Intuitive Explorations located in the back of the book.
2. When your energy is set for exploration, use all your cornerstone senses to see, hear, feel and just know the many paths that represent your unique potentials.
3. Take your time and note the types of trails you see, being aware of any that stand out more than the others.
4. Focus on the direction calling your attention most and observe its design.

5. Now follow the path and let it reveal to you a landscape or scene. Give yourself plenty of time to watch events unfold without wondering what they mean. Witness the scene like a movie, following the story and anticipating its outcomes and messages.

When you have finished this purposeful exploration, be the intuitive detective. Ask yourself the following questions to determine what opportunities your path revealed and how you can enact your higher plan:

- How many paths did I see as my potentials?
- What did those paths look like and what do they reveal about my soul's purpose?
- What path stood out to me most? Where did it lead?
- What story unfolded as I followed my path? What does this tell me about my potentials or need for healing?
- What would happen in my life today if I followed my unique path?
- How can I support my spirit's desires?

Support Your Sense of Purpose

When you find a path in life that suits your personal and collective desires, you have to be willing to follow it to fruition if you truly want to live a purposeful, not to mention fulfilling, life. However, in a culture that values money over experience, it can be difficult to march to your own beat. Below are a few ways to take strides toward breaking your rote cultural programming so that you can support the lifestyle that fits you best.

1. Don't be afraid to sample many options. In our society, there is little room for exploring opportunities. By the time you are eighteen, you're expected to know what you want in life. Yet in my experience, people don't truly grow up until they are in their forties. It seems restrictive and unrealistic to think we should have to have life figured out before that. If you didn't received permission to explore

many options in life, give yourself that gift today. Engage in all the things you enjoy until you find the one that sets your heart soaring.

2. Be creative and figure out how you can create your desires. Consider scaling back your lifestyle, getting renters to supplement your income, or seeking the help of others to create your purpose. You can solicit referrals, ask the people in your life to arrange blind dates for you, or find crowdfunding to launch your ideas. The point is to get innovative with your time and resources to generate the support necessary to achieve your goals.

3. Take action toward your purpose. You don't have to work hard, but you can work smart. Put in the physical, mental, emotional and spiritual time necessary to accomplish your ambitions. I know many spiritually-minded individuals who believe that if a relationship or endeavor becomes difficult to achieve, that means it's not meant to be, as if everything in life should be effortless. I don't agree with that philosophy. I think it's a fine line. There is a time to recognize when struggle is necessary for overcoming obstacles designed to grow you, just as there is a time when unnecessary effort keeps you tied to limiting patterns. Only you can know when to be persistent in an endeavor versus when to release it. Just be sure you don't fall into the trap of thinking that the universe will bring you what you need to survive without taking a physical action yourself. You need to apply effort in order for the universe to help you manifest your desires in the real world rather than only in your head.

4. Create rituals to support your purpose. Once a week, visualize yourself in your ideal lifestyle. Put money into a savings account at every full moon to afford your desires. Maybe even make a daily habit of taking one action, big or small, toward your purpose. Ritual is a great way to build energy for manifesting your dreams. Be creative.

Evolve Your Thinking

Of course, it's always worth considering the thoughts you have about your sense of soul purpose. Listen for the thoughts that move through your mind sounding like this: "I can't make money and do what I love," "I don't have a purpose," or "I don't want to do anything but watch television." Change those thoughts to match your higher truths. You can use the thoughts below to replace your own, or feel free to create new mantras.

> *"Life isn't about making money; it's about enjoying my experiences."*

> *"My purpose can be anything I choose."*

> *"It's healthy for me to take action toward creating a meaningful life."*

Intuition's Ability to Change the American Status Quo

When people come to see me for an intuitive session, one of the first things they most want to know is what their purpose is in life. While it is certainly noble to want to be a doctor, teacher or mother, the answer is never about a role one assumes. Purpose is a state of mind. You know you've achieved it when your spirit feels good about its life and about how it contributes to the greater good of all.

Any life expression that brings you joy and gives others happiness is a worthy pursuit. However, in a culture that values money over experience, our reasons for being distort. Suddenly, we believe fame and fortune bring fulfillment, never caring how it affects the world. Unfortunately, instant gratification never sates the soul and is a major contributor to the world's problems. Perhaps every American should make reinventing our ways of living a purpose today.

It is widely known that America's consumption rates are astronomical in comparison to other countries. In fact, Americans make up only 4.5% of the world's population yet consume nearly 20% of its energy. In an article by

Scientific America entitled, "Use It and Lose It: The Outsize Effect of U.S. Consumption on the Environment,"[xiv] Sierra Club's Dave Tilford states, "A child born in the United States will create thirteen times as much ecological damage over the course of his or her lifetime than a child born in Brazil." Tilford goes on to say, "With less than five percent of world population, the U.S. uses one-third of the world's paper, a quarter of the world's oil, twenty three percent of the coal, twenty seven percent of the aluminum, and nineteen percent of the copper." He also reports that, "Our per capita use of energy, metals, minerals, forest products, fish, grains, meat, and even fresh water dwarfs that of people living in the developing world."

The statistics above prove that in a world built on capitalism, two things become our life's philosophy and focus: acquiring money and consuming goods. We may not be a nation formed by religious ideology, yet we've certainly made working and shopping a doctrine. Too bad we never considered the consequences our pursuit of meaningless things would have on our bodies, minds and spirits, not to mention the environment.

Furthermore, it would seem that our excessive need for money and things isn't making us happier or healthier. In fact, anxiety disorders now affect 40 million adults in the United States. The Surgeon General reports that nearly 21 million people have medically diagnosed substance abuse disorders.[xv] According to the American Psychological Association, forty to fifty percent of married couples in the United States divorce.[xvi] And you only have to turn on the news to know that gun violence in our schools is occurring with staggering frequency. It would seem that the American ideal of buy and spend does not make for contented individuals. Thankfully, your intuition offers you a purpose and a new solution to updating the American agenda.

One of the keys to changing the world is using intuition to discover higher ways of being that celebrate humanity, earth and all living things, which, thankfully, is already happening. There are higher ideals we can follow that have the potential to set a new standard of living in America. For instance, using the power of your dollar to support ideals like wind and solar renewable energies, community vegetable gardens at every public school, eliminating packaging and processed food from store shelves, getting rid of pesticides that kill bees, converting to electric cars, establishing B-Corporations, Share Economies, or investing in Change Finance funds that "enable investors to drive impact, creating an economy in service to life through financial activism."

Capitalism doesn't have to change, we just need businesses that care more about people and the planet rather than profits and bottom lines. Follow your higher promptings, and put an end to frivolous lifestyles that are unconscious of the bigger picture. Get involved in creating a brighter future by lending your intuitive thinking to ideas that benefit humanity and Mother Earth.

Heal Intimacy and Establish Gender Equality

"There is always some madness in love, but there is also always some reason in madness."

– Friedrich Nietzsche, Philosopher

SOPHIE HAD DIVORCED her self-absorbed husband ten years earlier. Wasting no time, she put herself back on the relationship market. She created profiles on dating sites and made a point to be social. She even asked friends to set her up on blind dates. However, no man seemed interested. Before she knew it, a decade had passed. Still single, she wondered if she would ever have a committed relationship again.

Each relationship you engage in is a soul-mate relationship, regardless of whether they become your spouse or nemesis. Keeping in mind that soul mates may assume a negative stance in order to prompt growth, it becomes necessary to discern the difference so that you don't inadvertently commit needless time to a lesson. Sophie would need to be aware of how her past union was aiding her so that she could release her fears about partnership and allow a different type of man into her life today.

When viewing relationship and intimacy issues, I use mirrors as my symbol. Mirrors allow you to see what another person is showing you about yourself that you may be unable to perceive. Observing Sophie's relationship mirror, I saw that her ex-husband reflected a young soul with a self-absorbed, devil-may-care attitude. I could also see a past lifetime between the couple when Sophie had been her ex-husband's mother, a persona she often slipped into when attempting to change his ways. This image intuitively told me that Sophie's marriage was revealing where she was out of balance spiritually and emotionally by overly nurturing souls who willfully chose lower expressions. By offering her the perspective of overt selfishness, Sophie's husband was helping her see where she was being excessively selfless – the reverse image of her husband.

Like most people, Sophie grew up believing that it is nobler to give than receive. She was in the habit of putting the needs of others before her own. Yet intuition would have you put yourself first at times as a means of establishing a healthy balance in your life. Selflessness is no better than selfishness. You simply have to know when to apply one versus the other as personal equilibrium demands.

Through intuitive perspective, it's easy to see that Sophie's ex-husband was acting as her soul mate by agreeing to help her recognize the limiting pattern that her sacrificial stance was creating in her life. By showing her how to be more self-concerned, Sophie could free herself from her lower experiences. Of course, relationships are always a two-way street. Sophie was also agreeing to be a soul mate to her husband. Her mirror was reflecting his transposed need to put others before self in order to achieve his soul's evolution. However, it wasn't Sophie's job to make her former spouse understand this reflective concept as he likely wouldn't hear it. Sophie only needed to use the insight to transform herself.

Yet, Sophie had another issue with attracting a partner that was more complex than just balancing her dichotomy between self and others. Sophie suffered from the same identity crisis as most women, both seeking and in relationship. When I first saw Sophie's mirror, I curiously noticed that she resembled a man more than a woman, although her physical appearance certainly said otherwise. This told me that Sophie was likely relying on her masculine nature more than her feminine.

As a soul, you are multidimensional. Energetically, you have a higher and lower self; a past, present and future self; a physical, mental, emotional, and spiritual self; a plethora of archetypal selves; and a masculine and feminine self, all of which need attention in order to maintain proper balance. While there is nothing wrong with male energy, Sophie was relying on her masculine essence to attract to her a man she hoped would celebrate her as a woman. Do you see the problem?

Many if not most women rely on their masculine nature in their lives more than their feminine. Historically, women have endured the marginalization of their gender. As a result, we've learned to match our counterparts, taking on their representation of separation, individuality and survival of the fittest. Unfortunately, the trade-off for our need to be like men just to survive is that we have lost touch with our feminine representations of connection, unity and vulnerability - in other words, all the things we want our men to cherish in us as women. It's no wonder that it can be difficult to find a suitable partner, let alone sustain a balanced relationship.

Interestingly, Sophie commented that she didn't really enjoy being a woman who wore dresses, jewelry and makeup. She preferred pants, simplicity and a low maintenance lifestyle. She also shared that it was very easy for her to assume the traditional masculine roles of working, paying the bills, and making decisions. Sophie was comfortable in her masculine stance and didn't want to be perceived as the weaker sex. In truth, she had forgotten what it was like to be a woman.

I quickly assured Sophie that being feminine would not weaken her, nor would it require her to develop a love for frilly things and a dependency on a man. I further explained that on a dualistic planet where there is night and day, up and down, and masculine and feminine, it's our job to balance our dichotomies so that we can establish harmony in all our relationships. What I have found is that the key to intimate relating is not to identify as one gender but to recognize when to assert either nature as situations demand. Sophie didn't need to deny her masculine survival instincts, she simply needed to integrate more of her feminine abilities of vulnerability and trust into the mix. This shift in perspective and attitude would be the magnetic attracter she needed to meet a quality partner.

Unfortunately, most people, men included, have experienced letdown, betrayal, and manipulation in partnership and, therefore, echo defensiveness rather than openness. The simple energetic repositioning between fear and love makes all the difference in who you draw to you emotionally, as well as how you sustain love. I personally believe that both men and women should assume a feminine posture when they want to attract or repair a relationship, as femininity carries the receptive element and masculinity the resistant.

If Sophie wanted a man to honor her as a woman, she would need to be open and be willing to explore just as much as needing to be independent, strong and assured. Remember, she wasn't giving up one thing for another, she was finding balance. If a potential relationship became dishonoring, she could always assert her masculine traits and separate from the situation.

Everyone has individual fears, wounds and insecurities that they need to overcome in order to grow as individuals and as partners. Some of that growth you achieve on your own while other times you can only learn to evolve with the help of another. Let's adventure into your past relationships and current beliefs about love, intimacy and union so that you can find greater personal balance and collective unity.

Explore Your Relationship Lessons

Relationships are mirrors showing you the areas in which your life needs development. It's wise to engage in partnerships and friendships. As you begin to see others as a form of self-reflection, you start to understand that there are two primary reasons soul mates enter into your life. They are either showing you a dualistic opposite of yourself that you are resistant toward and need to reverse to whatever degree is correct for you, or they are portraying a higher characteristic that you need to embrace more within yourself, again to the level that is best for you. Follow the exercise below to gain understanding of your relationship patterns so you can integrate new ways of relating to yourself and your partner.

1. Start by using the Standard Preparation for All Intuitive Explorations to once again, establish your discovery space.
2. When you have completed the steps in the preparation, use g your cornerstone senses and ask to have reflected to you the primary image you present in relationship. Take time to observe your image and what influence it is having on you as a romantic partner.
3. After studying your personal expression, recall a past relationship. See yourselves as reflections of one another. Notice the attitude you assume as well as the behaviors your partner emanates. Take note of the patterns that dominate the scene.

When you have intuitively viewed your mirrors, decode their meanings and find solutions to your relationship dilemmas.

- What primary nature do I present in partnership?
- How does my current stance affect my ability to love and be loved?
- Is there a healthier persona I can enact in relationship? How would my life differ if I changed my reflection?
- What was I reflecting to my partner from the past? How did my image aid my partner's growth?
- What was my former partner mirroring to me? What lessons did my soul mate teach me? Am I enacting those lessons in my life?
- What can I do right now to attract in or heal my current relationship based on what I witnessed in this exploration?

Maintain A Healthy Sense of Commitment

If you haven't noticed, creating your ideal partnership has nothing to do with changing your appearance; rather it's about recognizing your personal motivations. In other words, weight, money and status have little to do with finding or maintaining intimacy. It's whether your soul is driven by karmic fear or excitement that determines what you experience in relationship.

Be sure you listen to your spirit and not your ego. You'll know the difference, because ego will tell you to lose twenty pounds, while spirit will advise you to buy a flattering dress. The following points will help you ingrain or release the patterns you need in order to maintain a healthy sense of commitment.

1. Remember that both you and your mate have individual soul histories that influence how you relate. Be sure to avoid falling into old scenarios no longer relevant today. Don't parent your wife because you were her father in the past. Be her equal today in accordance with the roles you designed for yourselves in this lifetime. Be willing to acknowledge your shortcomings, and be committed to healing them. You are always evolving some aspect of yourself. It's perfectly acceptable to have flaws.

2. Don't expect your partner to be something you don't want to be for yourself. In other words, if you fear making money, your partner cannot take that on for you. You must overcome whatever your personal issues are in order to evolve.

3. Recognize that distance can be good. Partnerships are healthiest when they have independence as well as unity.

4. Realize that one person cannot be everything to you. Friends are just as important as intimate partnerships. Engage in many types of relationships, for instance, with tennis buddies, your intuitive development tribe, writing groups, yoga pals, etc. as this will advance your fulfillment quicker than anything.

5. Lastly, you cannot change others; you can only transform yourself and your perception of a situation. Avoid the need to alter your partner's behaviors. Provide the bigger picture, but allow them to do what they need to do with the information on their own timeframes.

Evolve Your Thinking

Now is the time you will want to create new mantras to support your new understandings. Isolate the words in your head that echo these principles, "There are no good people in the world," "I have to change to be received in love," or "Love never lasts." Shift those thoughts to higher concepts. Rid yourself of these negative thoughts by instituting the phrases below or anything that works best for you.

"The world is full of worthy people and I will find the one that is best for me."

"I'm perfect as I am, and my partner accepts all of me."

"Relationships grow me. I enjoy engaging with others."

How Intuition is Forming the Future of Women and Men

One of the most striking trends changing the world today is how women are speaking up about sexual assault, discrimination, and indifference of all kind. In biblical proportions, women of all backgrounds, colors, and beliefs are serving as the trumpet to blow down Jericho's walls today.

With the power of their voices and by marching through the streets, they are taking command and laying to rubble the oppressive structures that have kept them down. As we witness and partake in these women's movements, we are adhering to our collective mindset that has re-orientated toward intuitive thinking. As a result, more women are finding the power to speak their truths and step into their elevated positions.

However, we can condemn the masculine all we want for its patriarchal abuse, but when it comes right down to it, intuition also tells us that we are all in this together. Women and men need to learn to work in tandem if we truly desire balance, equality and peace in the world.

Remember, your soul has been both masculine and feminine, and it has run the gamut of experiences from victim to aggressor. What if someone we would call a sexual predator today had been, in fact, a helpless child subject to horrific atrocities and abuse in a past life? Furthermore, what if you had been their abuser? How would that greater awareness make you feel about that person and yourself in present time?

To think that your soul has not assumed a negative stance at some point in its history would be a denial. The truth is, male or female, we have all contributed to the unhealthy state of the world at one time or another. When we each take full accountability for that fact, a higher sense of justice ensues that accommodates healing, reformation and equality.

It is no longer men against women or women against men. There is a need for us all to recognize that both genders have endured the indoctrination of generational programming about what constitutes a man and a woman. We have all been playing out these archaic and oppressive expect-ations for eons, unconscious of their insidious implications. However, with our evolution into higher intuitive awareness, we can now realize that we have all been misled and, consequently, all suffer from deep imbalance and wounding. Every person needs healing and consideration today.

Thanks to intuition, the future female is one who knows herself, inwardly and outwardly. She is personally aware and serves as the higher voice of reason, the nurturer of innovation and the cultivator of compassion and acceptance. As a culture, we should support our women by investing in them as leaders in home, community, business and politics.

Thanks to intuition, the future male is one who knows himself inwardly and outwardly. He does not repress his emotions and works with all natures of himself. Culturally, we should be supporting our men by encouraging them to explore their deeper nature and by giving them permission for their alternative roles.

As we use our intuitive perspective to find forgiveness for our collective past, and as we allow love to transmute our anger and move us into higher expressions, men and women will once again learn to coexist in a garden of bliss.

You have now concluded all but one aspect of your journey into intuition. Continue using all the skills you have learned throughout this book in your everyday life. Remain aware by sensing your reality with your four cornerstone instincts. Assume command over your energy and how you perceive your reality. Keep your four vital life foundations balanced. And stay aware of how your karma is playing out in your life so you can learn to be authentic with yourself, your family, in your sense of purpose and with your significant other. With your intuition intact, life can take on new forms that more than support your heart's desires.

PART VI

INTUITIVELY ETHICAL

Ethical Standards for Living in the Intuitive Age

"Each of us has a unique part to play in the healing of the world."

– Marianne Williamson, Spiritual teacher

IN JULY 2018, I read an article in The Daily Dot reporting on a woman, Lauren Taylor, and her account of using her telepathic intuitive skills to calm a mountain lion that had found its way into her home. Apparently, the large cat entered the house seeking asylum from nearby wildfires. Of course, Taylor exited the residence, never expecting that she would be leaving the mountain lion alone in her home for six hours.

During the cougar's stay, Taylor had several telepathic meeting of-the-minds with the feline while gazing directly into her eyes from behind the window. Interestingly, Taylor's intent to send images of love and acceptance to the cat in hopes of letting her know she was safe worked. Before she knew it, the animal was fast asleep, stretched out behind Taylor's couch.

Over the next six hours, as the cougar occasionally roused, Taylor would send intuitive images to her that she was protected, out of harm's way, and that there was no need for alarm. However, as night approached, Taylor decided to change her tactic. Here is her account of how she convinced the mountain lion to leave:

"It was just a couple hours to dawn and we needed to prompt her to leave without alarming her so much that she panicked. I sent telepathic pictures of the routes out of the house via open doors and the route out the backyard, across the creek, through an open field, and back up into the hills. We got guidance that the way to rouse her and get her to leave her safe spot behind the sofa without panicking was through drumming. We called in native ancestors' support and started drumming. She roused and knew just what to do… walking out through the open doors, through the yard, across the creek, and through the empty field behind us exactly as we had shown her."

Lauren Taylor is a hero! She demonstrates the incredible ability your intuition has in positively affecting change in the world so that all Earth's inhabitants can peacefully coexist. Now that you understand how intuition works to bring you and every living being on the planet healing, you will likely want to extend this knowledge beyond just healing yourself.

In an effort to have a greater impact in how life operates around you, you may feel the need to share your insights with other people. You may feel the need to tell those closest to you what you intuitively understanding about yourself or what you have discerned about the source and solution to their personal issues. You may even want others to validate your amazing intuitive prowess by sharing what you have discerned about other people's intimate details. Just keep in mind that while there are times when intuition can be your best friend, as was the case with Lauren Taylor, there are also moments when you should reserve from being intuitive.

As with every concept in this book, there is a balance to all things. There are times when your higher insights benefit the greater good and therefore should be expressed, and there are instances when your instinctive understandings can harm others and should therefore be withheld. While it's great to engage in the intuitive conversation, there are ethics you will want to be aware of and uphold so you don't inadvertently cross someone else's boundaries, creating unintended damage. These ethics will keep you safe as an intuitive while also looking out for the greater good of all.

Ethical Standard #1 - You Can Only Heal Yourself

As an intuitive, you have access to healing insights that can benefit you and others. However, it's vital to understand that you cannot heal another person; you can only transform yourself. Although you can see the cause of another person's stagnant energy and negative patterns, you cannot heal those aspects for them. That's their work if they so choose. It's like the saying, "You can lead a horse to water but you can't make her drink." You can share your higher perceptions with others, but refrain from trying to make them "get it" or follow your suggestions. In other words, don't call to see if they are adhering to your instructions. Also, don't feel the need to coddle them through their metamorphosis. Generally, when you overly invest yourself in someone else's healing, you slip into your ego and are then only seeking unhealthy attention and hindering them from taking charge of their reality.

You can influence others best by being in balance personally and, in so doing, serving as an example of what is possible. Try not to force your agenda on another person, lest you scare them away from the intuitive process. Lend your insights, step back and allow the people in your life to do what they will with your perceptions.

Ethical Standard #2 - You Must Have Permission

It is also critically important that you ask permission before intuitively interpreting another person's energy field. Everyone has the right to privacy. Just because you think you can sense their higher solutions doesn't mean you should, nor does it mean they are ready to receive the information. If you believe someone could benefit from your insight, ask for their permission before expressing your intuition – or better yet, wait until they approach you, seeking your perspective.

Ethical Standard #3 - Be Forthright with Your Knowledge

I've noticed a curious belief over the years of working as an intuitive. Many people automatically think that just because I'm psychic, I know all the secrets of the universe. While that's partly true, I certainly have access to infinite knowledge, that's also the problem, it's infinite. There is no way I could have all the secrets to anything especially considering that as a human, I'm only using 10 percent of my brain… well, maybe more if you factor in intuition… or perhaps intuition is even the key that unlocks the other 90 percent.

Regardless, there is a great deal to know about the universe, energy and intuition and we are only beginning to scratch the surface of our incredible capacities. The above subjects are masteries and take years, if not lifetimes, of intentional work to comprehend fully. For this reason, it's important that as an intuitive you be humble and not overstate your knowledge.

It is necessary for you to know where your intuitive information comes from and how to discern your personal wisdoms from that of other energies such as spirit guides and deceased relatives. You will want to continue your intuitive development to become more proficient with your higher aptitudes.

Ethical Standard #4 - Assume Intuitive Integrity

It is a good practice not to espouse yourself as better or more knowledgeable than others simply for being intuitive. Don't make yourself, or allow others to make you, their authority or guru. Everyone can enter that realm! Remember, intuitives provide insightful possibilities, potentials and opportunities, not doctrine. We are all our own authority, and we all have access to the same universal knowledge. Empower others to assume command of their circumstances, and avoid the need to feel superior.

Ethical Standard #5 - Allow Objectivity to Rule

The greatest asset intuitives possess is their ability to be objective. By removing your personal judgments or analysis, you are recognizing that every person has a right to his or her unique experiences. Never forget that there is great purpose in all circumstances and that objectivity will allow you to find the meaning. Always approach intuitive information with your neutrality and amusement, never assuming there is a right or wrong way of living. Endeavor to find the higher purpose in all things.

Ethical Standard #6 - Use Your Intuition Therapeutically

Intuition is a therapy, not a novelty. Your higher senses represent an intricate system that consistently provides you with the solutions to life's perplexing issues. Intuitives find those higher understandings in an effort to invoke healing and make the world a better place. When being intuitive, seek answers, not applause.

Ethical Standard #7 - When NOT to be Intuitive

I once had a family member ask me for my intuitive interpretation of an event in her life. Taking my role seriously, I centered myself and held my neutrality and amusement. However, after completing my profound assessment, my family member scoffed at me and said, "Maybe next time you'll give me a good reading." I was hurt. It seemed to me that I had given her an unbiased and excellent understanding of her situation that she simply didn't want to hear, nor for which she wanted to take responsibility. That was when I learned never to offer insight to family. The problem is that the people you are closest to may feel that you are manipulating them into doing what you think is best for them and not what is truly in their best interest.

Because it's easy to cross ethical lines, or to be perceived as crossing those lines, it is best to refrain from offering insight to your loved ones. You can talk about your theories and ideals with family, just don't feel the need to intuitively witness their energy or tell them how to solve their issues. Instead, encourage them to be intuitive for themselves. Help them learn the skills you have learned in this book so that they can heal themselves and find their own solutions.

Keep these seven intuitive ethical standards in the forefront of your mind as you begin to formulate a better world around you. Remember to assume your most authentic stance while also respecting that every person has the right to his or her own beliefs and timing. Simply be responsive to the needs of your higher self, and watch as the world automatically shifts to match you.

Intuitively Transforming the American Dream

"Choose always the way that seems the best, however rough it may be; custom will soon render it easy and agreeable."

– Pythagoras, Greek Philosopher[xvii]

CONGRATULATIONS! You've just earned your degree in how to be Intuitively You. This achievement is one of the greatest assets you will ever acquire. You now have the life skills necessary to achieve personal healing and sustainable well-being. As you live intuitively, experiencing improved health, increased wealth, deeper connections and higher purpose, your life will reflect your utmost joy and fulfillment. However, your journey need not end here. You can also work toward your mastery in intuition, which requires that you apply your higher senses as a means of transforming what we know to be the American Dream.

Our world is in dire need of reform. We continue to pollute our air, water and land, depleting our environment to the point of near collapse. Worse still, we treat each other with hatred and loathing, then wonder why our youth think it's acceptable to take up arms and march to their schools to make their point. Our destructive ways must end. After all, is this really the bleak future we want to perpetuate for our children? Of course not!

The vast majority of us don't agree with the way we live our lives. We are smart enough to understand that fossil fuels harm the earth, while wind and solar energies work in harmony with the environment. We know that processed, chemically-treated and modified foods cause cancer, autoimmune diseases and a whole host of other physical ailments. And to be sure, we are critically aware that choosing money and meaningless things over time spent loving and raising our children has profoundly negative ramifications on the psyche of a growing mind.

It's easy to see what fixes the issues. Unfortunately, the daily lives we have built around our lower ideals makes us feel trapped. We believe we are unable to make a difference, and so rather than resist, we go along with society's false sense of expectation. However, a new era of enlightenment is upon us. Individuals like you now have a green light to transform what has become an outdated American agenda.

Many eons ago, ancient philosophers such as Plato and Pythagoras foretold of a nation that would one day provide all matters of human need physically, mentally, emotionally and spiritually. This country would set a higher standard for uniting its people under the umbrella of understanding and acceptance for ALL regardless of gender, color, creed or sexual orientation. Furthermore, this nation would offer peace to all other nations, unifying them globally for the greater good of all. Can you imagine the lives we will live when this vision comes to fruition? If that sounds too good to believe, think again.

The time is now, the nation is the United States, and WE THE PEOPLE will set the example for peace in the world.

I can complain about how far our country has strayed from its originating ideals, but when it comes right down to it, Americans are still exceptionally privileged. We are fortunate to have free speech and a constitution that supports individual need over governmental desire. This begs the question, "Why haven't we created peace in the world yet?" Because the real key to creating a balanced and thriving democracy is to combine our right to speak along and our command of rule with our intuitive higher knowledge and its ability to solve a perplexing problem.

Reforming the American ideal is not the job of our corporations and government. We are a nation of the people by the people. Transforming our lifestyles is the responsibility of every American and as an intuitive, pioneering spirit, you are the forerunner of this grand revolution.

Your newfound higher thoughts will sow the seeds that will transform our nation. And you are not alone. Swarms of people like you are waking up and realizing that through the metaphysical and quantum sciences, a new world can form – a better world. All that you, as an individual, have to do to achieve this higher goal are four simple things, one of which you've already accomplished by reading and implementing the concepts in this book.

1. Gain your intuitive understanding. As you now know, intuition is the ultimate life cure. Your circumstances will only truly change when you shift into a higher perspective. Share this understanding with whoever can hear it. Consider how intuition can be taught to our children in school and in all educational courses related to health and human study.

2. Find your intuitive tribe and combine your higher ideals on how to solve our collective life issues. Discuss your thoughts on creating environmentally and sustainable free-energy sources with each other. Talk about how to live locally and develop health care systems in your communities that every individual can easily access and which combine traditional and alternative medicines to advance all aspects of healing. Think of all the ways in which your community can be healthier, more sustaining and environmentally friendly by putting your mind to changing your immediate region.

3. Speak out on behalf of the greater good using your intuitive voice of neutrality and amusement. Let your corporate executives and government representatives know the type of lifestyle you want to live rather than allowing them to tell you what you want. If you desire a world in which people and the planet take precedence over profit, peacefully send a message to the world's conglomerates by not purchasing their products if they support lower ways of being.

If you want a world in which individuality and difference are celebrated, tell your elected officials through your vote how to carry out your higher standards. Remember your American privileges and don't forget that you are in command. Exercise your American rights and voice your opinion.

4. Don't settle for less. Intuition is the great balancing force. When you operate from your higher self, you always want what is best not just for yourself but for everyone. Be willing to peacefully express what is fair for all, and don't back down until you've achieved your higher goal.

As you go forward with your intuition intact, know that Earth is an ever-abundant garden waiting to sprout at your command. She looks forward to our peaceful evolution. Just don't make it harder than it needs to be. Do something small daily by using your cornerstone senses, assume your energetic responsibilities, heal your relationships to self and others, and watch as life bends to your higher will as you transform the American Dream.

Standard Preparation for All Intuitive Explorations

1. Begin by closing your eyes, or inwardly focusing, and placing your awareness in your center-of-head Command Central, making sure no one is in your headquarters but you.

2. Once your Command Central is clear, intend that you be grounding to the earth in present time. Simply envision a column, or cord, that extends from your hips all the way to the core of the Earth, consciously grounding your body, mind and spirit in the here and now.

3. When you are connected to the present moment, claim your energy field by first putting yourself in a bubble and defining where your energy starts and stops.

4. Next, place a symbolic boundary around yourself, establishing your sense of authority. Remember you can use anything you like for boundaries such as flowers, crystals or light but intend that it keep you safe and in charge of your exploration.

5. Once you have your field anchored, defined and protected, renew your energies so you are clear when conducting your intuitive explorations.

6. To clear your field, intend that your grounding cord be open, or hollow on the inside, and command that all the energy in your field

release down your grounding cord and into the Earth where it will be filtered and recycled back into a state of optimal use. Be sure to let go of everyone including children and loved ones. Release your projects, ideas, hopes and fears and allow yourself to come into a state of nothingness, where all is in divine order.

7. Enjoy the stillness for a moment, knowing that all your potentials and opportunities exist in this vast universal expanse. Breathe in your desires, ideas, and solutions without having to know what they are or how to manifest them, that will come in time, but for now *be* in alignment with all that is, and can be.

8. When you have taken a moment for release and stillness, you can reinvigorate your field by calling back to you the energy you sent out to be renewed.

9. Envisioning a large golden sun above your head, intend that all the energy you released into the Earth for clearing now be sent into your sun where it will complete its recycling process. Watch as your symbolic sun grows and expands as your energy filters in and combines with the sun's limitless perspectives, ideas and opportunities.

10. When your sun is large and full of pure potential, pop it like a balloon, filling yourself in with the sun's warming light, head to toe, fully absorbing the radiant energy, as you allow it to empower you with the ability to create your greatest desires.

11. Once you are fully empowered, intend that your halo, or crown, be set to the unique colors for you that represent neutrality and amusement.

12. After defining the higher awareness you will use to approach your discovery, you can activate your inner viewing screen and begin your intuitive exploration.

ENDNOTES

[i] Lewis Bostwick, Berkley Psychic Institute, http://www.berkeleypsychic. com/ShowPage.asp?id=163

[ii] Bruce Kasanof, "Intuition is the Highest Form of Intelligence," *Forbes*, February 21, 2017.

[iii] Michio Kaku, *Strings, Conformal Fields, and M-theory*, Edition 2 (NY: Springer,1999).

[iv] Artistotle, 323 BC.

[v] Lynne McTaggart, *The Field*, from her epilogue, "The Coming Revolution," NY: HarperCollins, 2002.

[vi] J. S. Lundeen, A. M. Steinberg, "Experimental Joint Weak Measurement on a Photon Pair as a Probe of Hardy's Paradox," Physical Review Letters 102: 020404–000001, 2009. doi:10.1103/ PhysRevLett.102.020404

[vii] Masaru Emoto, *The Hidden Messages In Water* (Oregon: Beyond Worlds Publishing, 2004).

[viii] "70,000 Thoughts a Day Myth?" *Neuroskeptic*, May 9, 2012.

[ix] William Schutz, Joy: *Expanding Human Awareness*, 1967.

[x] H. E. Puthoff, "CIA-Initiated Remote Viewing at Stanford Research Institute," Ph.D. Institute for Advanced Studies at Austin, TX 1995.

[xi] "The Reality of ESP: A Physicist's Proof of Psychic Abilities," Watkins *Mind Body Spirit*, 2015.

[xii] "Descartes and the Pineal Gland," First published Apr 25, 2005; substantive revision Sep 18, 2013, Stanford Encyclopedia of Philosophy.

[xiii] https://www.dalailama.com/the-dalai-lama/biography-and-daily-life/ reincarnation

[xiv] https://www.scientificamerican.com/article/ american-consumption-habits/

[xv] https://addiction.surgeongeneral.gov/sites/default/files/toolkit.pdf

[xvi] http://www.apa.org/topics/divorce/

[xvii] Stanford Encyclopedia of Philosophy, "Pythagoras"

CPSIA information can be obtained
at www.ICGtesting.com
Printed in the USA
FSHW011857030419
56926FS